Upon Further Reflection

Upon Further Reflection

B. F. Skinner

PRENTICE-HALL, INC., Englewood Cliffs, New Jersey 07632

Library of Congress Cataloging-in-Publication Data

Skinner, B. F. (Burrhus Frederic)
  Upon further reflection.

  (Century psychology series)
  Includes bibliographies and index.
  1. Psychology, Experimental—Addresses, essays,
lectures. 2. Human behavior—Addresses, essays,
lectures. I. Title. II. Series: Century psychology
series (Englewood Cliffs, N.J.)
BF181.S63 1987   150.19'434   86-550
ISBN 0-13-938986-5

Editorial supervision
  and interior design by **Lisa Halttunen**
Manufacturing buyer: **Barbara Kelly Kittle**

Printed in the United States of America
10 9 8 7 6 5 4 3 2

0-13-938986-5 01

Prentice-Hall International (UK) Limited, *London*
Prentice-Hall of Australia Pty. Limited, *Sydney*
Prentice-Hall Canada Inc., *Toronto*
Prentice-Hall Hispanoamericana, S.A., *Mexico*
Prentice-Hall of India Private Limited, *New Delhi*
Prentice-Hall of Japan, Inc., *Tokyo*
Prentice-Hall of Southeast Asia Pte. Ltd., *Singapore*
Editora Prentice-Hall do Brasil, Ltda., *Rio de Janeiro*
Whitehall Books Limited, *Wellington, New Zealand*

Contents

ईॐईॐईॐईॐईॐ

Preface

ﻉ﮲ﻉ﮲ﻉ﮲ﻉ﮲ﻉ﮲ﻉ﮲ﻉ﮲

Like *Reflections on Behaviorism and Society*, this is not a book to be read straight through. There is no central theme beyond the commitment to an experimental analysis of behavior and its use in the interpretation of human affairs. The book moves from the very general (the three chapters on global problems in Part I) to the very particular (the four chapters, for specialists only, on the experimental analysis of operant behavior in Part V). The three chapters in Part II analyze the role of selection by consequences in evolution and operant conditioning. The chapters in Part III are criticisms of the cognitive approach to human behavior in psychology and education. The chapters in Part IV apply an operant analysis to self-management in writing papers and growing old.

Because the papers were written to be read separately, they may be read in any order. There is some repetition, but none, I hope, beyond a helpful emphasis of a few basic points.

Professor Barbara Ross has done much to improve the ease with which these papers can be read and understood. I am greatly indebted to her for extensive editorial help. I also thank Jean Fargo and Judy Fahey for their part in the final word processing of the manuscript.

B. F. Skinner

chapter 1

Why We Are Not Acting to Save the World

੨ଈ੨ଈ੨ଈ੨ଈ੨ଈ.

Most thoughtful people agree that the world is in serious trouble. A nuclear war could mean a nuclear winter that would destroy all living things; fossil fuels will not last forever, and many other critical resources are nearing exhaustion; the earth grows steadily less habitable; and all this is exacerbated by a burgeoning population that resists control. The timetable may not be clear, but the threat is real. That many people have begun to find a recital of these dangers tiresome is perhaps an even greater threat.

Why is more not being done? Within a single generation, we have made extraordinary progress in the exploration of space, genetic engineering, electronic technology, and many other fields, but little has been done to solve what are certainly more serious problems. We know what could be done: We could destroy all nuclear weapons, limit family size, and adopt a much less polluting and less wasteful style of life. The mere listing of these steps is enough to show how far we are from taking them.

Traditional explanations of why we are doing so little are familiar. It is said that we lack responsibility for those who will follow us, that we do not have a clear perception of the problem, that we are not using our intelligence, that we are suffering from a failure of will, that we lack moral strength, and so on. Unfortunately, explanations of that sort simply replace one question with another. Why are we not more responsible or more intelligent? Why are we suffering from a failure of will? A better strategy is to look at our behavior and at the environmental conditions of which it is a function. There we shall find at least some of the reasons why we do as we do. They are also explanations of the bodily conditions we call feelings and states of mind.

The present problem then becomes clear: We are being asked to do something about the future. But the future does not exist. It cannot act upon us; we cannot act upon it. We speak of the future when we say that we act with a purpose— but purpose is no longer an acceptable scientific principle. Birds, for example, appear to build nests for the purpose of hatching and rearing their young. They certainly do build them and later use them, but we should not say that they build them *because of* the future use.

The concept of purpose has been replaced by that of *selection,* which was first recognized by Darwin and Wallace in the natural selection of species. Birds build nests not because of the nests' future usefulness but because variations in genetic structure that led them to build nests in slightly different ways were selected by the greater chance of survival of the species when that was done. A single instance of nestbuilding has a structure in which an action is followed by a consequence, but the consequence follows only because similar consequences have followed in the past. Our present problem arises because, although natural selection prepares a species for a future, it is only a future that resembles the selecting past. In a different environment, a species may perish.

That fault was to some extent corrected by the evolution of a process through which an individual organism could acquire behavior that was effective in environments too unstable for natural selection. This process, *operant conditioning,* is also a kind of selection, and it is not surprising that the behavior also appears to be purposive. It is sometimes called goal-directed, but a goal has no effect on the behavior through which it is reached or on the probability that the behavior will occur. Its effect is felt only on future instances. Our problem therefore persists: Operant behavior, like natural selection, prepares the organism for a future, but it is only a future that is similar to the selecting past. Moreover, the repertoire of behaviors that can be acquired without help by a single organism in a single lifetime is not very large.

That fault was in turn corrected by the evolution of processes through which organisms were affected by the selecting pasts of other members of the species. Imitation is an example. When members of a group imitate each other and model behavior to be imitated, they acquire much larger repertoires, which are effective under a greater variety of conditions. The human species went far beyond imitation and modeling with the evolution of verbal behavior, or language. People not only show each other what to do—they tell them.

A language is the product of a third kind of selection by consequences, the evolution of cultures. A culture evolves when new practices, introduced for perhaps irrelevant reasons, are selected by their contributions to the survival of the practicing group. Cultural practices are also said to have purposes. For example, the purpose of education is said to be the production of informed members of a group, but again, we should speak only of selecting consequences. Educational practices evolve when they contribute informed members to the group.

Education is also an example of two other faults that are relevant to our problem: (1) traits persist long after the conditions responsible for their selection have changed, and (2) the changes may have been caused by selected traits. Thus, the digestive system of a species and its ingestive behavior presumably evolved at the same time. In a stable environment, animals "instinctively" eat foods they can digest. That is due to natural selection. When, in addition, special susceptibilities to operant reinforcement by foodstuffs evolved, animals learned to find other foods that also met their nutritional needs. That was particularly important when essential foods were scarce. In the early history of the human species, for example, salt and sugar were almost always in short supply. A person in whom genetic change increased the susceptibility to reinforcement by salt and sugar must have learned more quickly and remembered longer where to find them. A trait evolved that gave the individual, and then the species, an important advantage, but it also caused trouble. Thanks to those very susceptibilities to reinforcement, people discovered and produced great quantities of salt and sugar. The susceptibilities survived, and we now eat much more salt and sugar than is good for us. The species created a world in which some of its genetic susceptibilities to reinforcement were out of date. Fortunately, another cultural practice helps: Medical scientists have discovered the harmful effects of too much salt and sugar and advise people to eat less of them. If the consequences were more serious, candy bars and bags of salted nuts would carry the warning, *The Surgeon General has determined that this product may be dangerous to your health.*

Two other susceptibilities have caused more of the trouble we are concerned with here. First, when the species was living in a far-from-hospitable world and was periodically decimated by famine and pestilence, it was important for people to breed as often as possible. A heightened susceptibility to reinforcement by sexual contact evolved, which is now responsible for the danger and misery of overpopulation. Second, when people protected themselves and their possessions in hand-to-hand combat, reinforcement by any sign that one had hurt one's opponent helped shape and maintain skillful fighting. A susceptibility to reinforcement evolved that has led to the invention and production of weapons that hurt much larger numbers of people in much more decisive ways.

It is often proposed that we solve these problems by warning people of the consequences of their behavior. "Raising consciousness" is the fashionable expression. It is implied that once people know that their behavior will have dangerous consequences, they will change. Such an appeal to knowledge has caused a great deal of trouble. A distinction is sometimes drawn between knowing what will happen when we act in a given way because certain consequences have followed when we have acted that way (in which case we are said to "know by acquaintance") and knowing because we have been told what will happen ("knowing by description"). What is missing in knowledge by description is a reason why we should act. If we borrow our friend's pen and enjoy writing with it, we may buy one like it. We know by acquaintance that it is a good pen. We buy it because positive reinforcement has been at work. If, instead, our friend simply tells us that it is a good pen, we know that fact by description, but we shall buy one only if we have already profitably followed our friend's advice or the advice of others with whom we have had similar experiences.

Obviously we cannot know the future by acquaintance, and we have very little reason to act because we know it by description. In general, the more remote the predicted consequences, the less likely we are to follow advice. We have more often been successful when we have followed advice about the immediate future because that kind of advice has been more often tested and found better. The advice we are now being offered is about a distant future; it may be good advice, but that has very little to do with whether we shall take it.

We are also not likely to take the kind of advice called a warning. When the predicted consequences of our behavior are punishing, we must prevent or escape from them. But it is often easier to escape in other ways—by ignoring or forgetting the advice or by finding a way to escape that does not require solving the problem. Recent apocalyptic thinking in America has taken the latter line. We are said to be in "the last days." Because our future lies in another world, this world is expendable. Nothing need be done about it.

We are also not likely to take the advice we are now being offered because the immediate consequences are punishing. The old susceptibilities to reinforcement are still with us, and the behavior they strengthen is naturally incompatible with any attempt to suppress it. It takes strong advice to induce most people to stop consuming irreplaceable resources, to moderate the joys of procreation and parenthood, and to destroy weapons that make them feel secure against their enemies. And there is another reason why knowledge about the future is not likely to solve our problem: To the extent that advice is not taken, it is not likely to be given.

It is true that advice about a personal future may be effective. Many people have stopped smoking, for example, and perhaps some of them have done so because they were told that it causes lung cancer. That is all the more significant because smoking is strongly reinforced, because the effects of stopping do not follow immediately, and because the advice can be dismissed as merely statistical ("Smoking doesn't cause cancer in everyone, and it won't in me"). But except for a few people who, like physicians, are accustomed to taking that kind of advice and seeing the consequences close at hand, most people have probably stopped for more immediate reasons—a rough throat or a cigarette cough, the annoying constraints of no-smoking signs, the protests of strangers, the condescending tolerance of friends who have stopped, the inflated cost of cigarettes, and so on.

That very fact may be helpful, however. Can something of the sort not be done to solve our problem? Why not arrange immediate consequences that will have the effect that remote consequences would have if they were acting now? There is nothing very new in that suggestion. Ethics is mainly a matter of the conflict between immediate and remote consequences. How can we forego a reward in order to avoid a later punishment or take punishment for the sake of a later reward? Cultures have helped to solve the problem by supplying immediate consequences that have the same effect as the remote ones. They shame their members who fail to forego immediate rewards or refuse to take immediate punishment, and commend those who do. If eating too much salt and sugar were more serious, it would be called shameful.

It might also be called illegal or sinful, because in advanced cultures sanctions of that sort are taken over by governments and religions. Those institutions outlive people, and those who respond to their sanctions can therefore be said to be working for a future beyond their own. The sanctions are usually punitive: One pays taxes to a government or contributes to a religion because punishment of some sort will follow if one does not. But positive consequences also usually follow—security and order in the case of government, and peace of mind and answers to puzzling questions in the case of religion. These positive consequences are sometimes called the justifications of governments and religions. Money and goods are other immediate reinforcers used to induce people to work for a future beyond their own—the future of a business or industry. The justification is said to be the more abundant production and distribution of goods. Without these so-called justifications, governments, religions, and capital would not have been able to maintain their control.

If the futures of governments, religions, and capitalistic systems were congruent with the future of the species, our problem would be solved. When a certain behavior was found to endanger the species, the institutions would declare it illegal, sinful, or too costly, respectively, and would change the contingencies they impose. Unfortunately, the futures are different. Nuclear weapons are made to guarantee the survival of governments and religions, not the species. Governments and religions estimate their strength in the sheer number of their supporters and are therefore "prolife." (China may seem to be an exception, but overpopulation was already severe; the future had arrived.) Governments and religions enlist support by defending the right to property and the pursuit of happiness, and it is only when a very near future threatens (for example, during a war) that they risk defection by imposing austerity.

Governments, religions, and capitalistic systems, whether public or private, control most of the reinforcers of daily life; they must use them, as they have always done, for their own aggrandizement, and they have nothing to gain by relinquishing power. Those institutions are the embodiments of cultural practices that have come into existence through selection, but the contingencies of selection are in conflict with the future of the human species.

The fact that selection by consequences prepares only for a future like the selecting past is a flaw that, as we have seen, has been successively corrected—the flaw in natural selection by operant conditioning and the flaw in operant conditioning by the evolution of cultural practices. But there is another possible step. Among evolved cultural practices are those of science, and with them we should be able to *intervene* in the process of selection. We should be able either to introduce variations (rather than wait for them to occur by chance) or to change the contingencies of selection. Something of the sort has long been done. For thousands of years, people have intervened in the evolution of domestic animals through selective breeding, and they can now do so with greater precision. For the first time it is possible to introduce variations by changing genes. People have always intervened in the development of personal repertoires of behavior either by introducing variations (as by modeling new kinds of behavior to be imitated) or by changing the contingencies of reinforcement. Programmed instruction does both. Only occasionally have people changed the contingencies of selection responsible for cultural practices (although they have sometimes done so to preserve a valued practice that was on the verge of extinction), but people routinely change cultures by introducing new practices as variations to be selected. Rather than wait for further variation and selection to solve our problem, can we not *design* a way of life that will have a better chance of a future?

Perhaps it is time to ask who "we" are. An answer may be found simply by listing those who are now most active in considering the problem. For the most part, *we* are scholars, scientists, teachers, and writers for the media. We are the uncommitted—to governments, religions, and capital—and are therefore free to consider a more remote future. But we are free only to the extent that we are indeed uncommitted. If among us there are leaders in government, religion, and business, they are with us only to the extent that they are uncommitted to their respective institutions.

Those of us who are scientists can give the best picture of the future, and it need not resemble the selecting past. Much of science is simply a record of what has happened (it is knowledge by acquaintance), but much is also knowledge by description. By analyzing a complex system and applying what has already been learned about its parts, scientists predict events that have never occurred before. By examining a chain of gears, for example, we can say that if gear A is turned clockwise, gear H will turn counterclockwise, even though we have not yet seen it do so. We can also construct a chain in which a given gear will turn in a given way. The prediction and construction of a rather more important chain of events were confirmed at Alamagordo.

We are concerned here, however, with chains involving people rather than gears or nuclei, and much of what we learn will depend upon the competence of those of us who are behavioral scientists. Do we know enough about simple arrangements of variables to predict the effects of novel arrangements? What facts about experienced cases will tell us what we need to know about the unexperienced?

Much of what is called behavioral science—political science, economics, anthropology, and sociology—is confined to what people have done throughout history or are doing now in the environments in which they live. It is knowledge by acquaintance. With one exception, the same can be said of psychology, which has turned more and more to case histories, questionnaires, inventories, and other records of what people have said and done. The behavior studied by all these sciences is the product of the genetics of the species and of past or present cultures. Moreover, the behavioral scientists are themselves the products of their cultures. As it is often said, they are not free of ideology.

The exception just noted is the experimental analysis of behavior. It is seldom invoked in discussions of the world at large—ironically, for reasons that are in fact its strength, particularly with respect to the present problem. Because it has for the most part studied nonhuman animals, the experimental analysis of behavior is said to neglect all that is essentially human. Because it has been most successful in studying the behavior of nonverbal human subjects—young children or the retarded or psychotic—it is said to neglect cognitive skills. But there are reasons for those strategies. In any field of science, one begins with facts that can be predicted and controlled with some precision and then moves on to more complex facts only when the increasing power of the analysis permits. Where prediction and control are not yet possible, one must turn to interpretation. That is standard scientific practice. Most of the facts of evolution, for example, are out of reach of prediction and control. The theory of evolution is an inter-pretation, but it is strongly supported by a science in which prediction and control are possible—the science of genetics. The experimental analysis of behavior is the "genetics" of the behavioral sciences.

There is another reason why most scientific accounts of human behavior remain a matter of interpretation. The species is distinguished by the fact that its members engage in verbal behavior. They not only *respond* to contingencies of reinforcement as rats and pigeons do; they *talk* about them. They formulate rules and give each other, and themselves, advice. They are taught to do so at an early age and continue to do so throughout their lives. In any given setting, therefore, whether in daily life or the laboratory, human behavior must be treated as a joint product of the prevailing contingencies of reinforcement and of what a person says about them. That does not mean that human behavior is not lawful, because we should be able to account for it if we knew all the facts, but most of what people tell themselves about the world in which they live is a product of a personal history that is out of our reach. For a long time to come, human behavior will probably remain largely a subject for interpretation rather than for prediction and control. Hence we can see the importance of a science that studies the behavior of organisms whose basic behavioral processes are free of verbal complications—that is, non-verbal species or human subjects who have not acquired extensive verbal behavior.

An analogy may be useful. Suppose that the human species developed an organ in addition to the lungs that helped in the exchange of gases with the environment. Then, in order to discover how the lungs worked, we should have to find a person in whom the other organ had not evolved, had been lost, or could be temporarily put out of action. Or we should have to study the lungs of other species. Verbal behavior has the effect of such an organ: The basic behavioral processes can be studied without confusion only when it is out of action. However, verbal behavior itself can be analyzed in the same terms.

Another feature of the experimental analysis of behavior is relevant. Early experiments on animal behavior were almost always designed to test theories. The theories were usually drawn from the personal histories of the experimenters. The results were therefore not free of ideology. The experimental analysis of behavior, however, uses very little theory beyond the assumption of lawfulness in its subject matter. It moves on to the study of new properties of behavior as they turn up one after another as the research proceeds. The result is therefore as free as possible of the ideology of the scientist.

If human nature means the genetic endowment of the species, we cannot change it. But we have the science needed to design a world that would take that nature into account and correct many of the miscarriages of evolution. It would be a world in which people treated each other well, not because of sanctions imposed by governments or religions but because of immediate, face-to-face consequences. It would be a world in which people produced the goods they needed, not because of contingencies arranged by a business or industry but simply because they were "goods" and hence directly reinforcing. It would be a beautiful and interesting world because making it so would be reinforced by beautiful and interesting things. It would be a world in which the population was kept at a safe level because all social and economic incentives for having children had been removed and conception was easily preventable or freely revokable. It would be a world in which the social and commercial practices that promote unnecessary consumption and pollution had been abolished. It would be a way of life that would give the species a much longer lease on the planet Earth. It could all be done without "raising consciousness." *Only those who designed the relations between behavior and its consequences would need to take the remoter consequences into account.*

What are the chances that a culture so designed could take over? It could not simply be imposed, of course. It would not be the right culture if that were done. Nor could it escape from selection by consequences. New practices would appear as variations, to survive only if they contributed to the strength of the group. The practices mentioned above would obviously run into trouble. They would be opposed by the institutions they were designed to replace. Even if the changes were carefully programmed and moved only slowly in the right direction, they would be resisted as soon as it was clear that they threatened governments, religions, and economic enterprises. Nor would it be possible to turn to the people for support, because they would also be the products of earlier cultures. A designed way of life would be liked by those who lived it (or the design would be faulty), but it would almost certainly not appeal to those who like what they like because they have been taught to like it by a different culture.

The power of the uncommitted lies not only in science but in education and counseling. The uncommitted work slowly, however, and our problem seems to demand immediate action. Faced with the indescribable dangers of nuclear war, it seems irresponsible simply to teach young people the ultimate futility of violence. Faced with the unspeakable misery of overpopulation, it seems irresponsible simply to teach young people the satisfactions to be found in a small family or a childless life. Faced with the prediction of what life will be like when critical resources are nearly exhausted and the environment irreversibly polluted, it seems irresponsible simply to teach young people to enjoy themselves in less threatening ways. But building a new culture from the very beginning may be our only hope.

We may find some consolation in the fact that no true intervention is possible. We cannot step into the history of life on Earth as if we were not part of it. If people have ever changed the course of evolution, they have done so because evolved cultural practices made it possible. If we cannot intervene, however, we can at least watch. Are there signs, for example, that institutions are growing weaker? Certainly there is no clear move toward a government that governs best because it governs least. Religion is playing a more important role than it has played for some time, and it has turned again to more violent measures. Business and industry have scarcely narrowed the gap between the rich and the poor of the earth.

Conflicts between institutions are a large part of the trouble, but there is little evidence that they are being resolved. The League of Nations that emerged from the horrors of the First World War grew weaker as the war was forgotten. The United Nations that followed an even more horrible war has grown weaker as memories of the conflict have faded. Ecumenical movements in religion do not go far beyond proselytizing. Competition is still the lifeblood of business and industry, and we are far from a common world market. In short, those who control the contingencies of reinforcement under which we all live show little sign of relinquishing their power for the sake of the species.

Nothing much more promising is to be said for the uncommitted. Many organizations are dedicated to the prevention of nuclear war, overpopulation, and the exhaustion and destruction of a livable environment, but their protests are necessarily directed toward governments, religions, and economic systems, and there they stop. Moreover, the principal modus operandi of these organizations is to frighten people rather than offer them a world to which they will turn because of the reinforcing consequences of doing so.

If the evidence survives, visitors from outer space may some day reconstruct a curious story. The Earth was a small planet, but it proved suitable for life. At some point atoms came together in a molecule that, under just the right conditions, reproduced itself. Random variations in the structure of that molecule made reproduction possible under less favorable circumstances. Cells evolved and then organs, organisms, and species. Interchanges with the environment became more and more complex. In one species, *Homo sapiens,* the vocal musculature came under operant control and people began to talk to each other and exchange experiences. Elaborate cultural practices evolved, among them science and technology. Unfortunately, they were used to support genetic dispositions that had evolved at an earlier stage. Because food was reinforcing, people raised, stored, and distributed vast quantities of it. Because moving about was useful and exciting, they invented trains, cars, airplanes, and spaceships. Because good things could be taken from other people and then needed to be defended, they invented clubs, guns, and bombs. Because they wished to avoid ill health and the threat of death, they practiced medicine and sanitation. They lived longer and their numbers increased, and they took over more and more of the Earth and brought it under cultivation. They consumed more and more of its irreplaceable resources. In the struggle for what was left, they began to build weapons so powerful that they could bring life on Earth to an end.

A few people saw the danger and worried about it, but their proposals conflicted with practices that were supported not only by immediate and hence more powerful consequences but by the out-of-date moral and ethical principles that had been invented to justify them. Those who were able to do so continued to breed at will, consume without restraint, and prepare to defend themselves at any cost. Eventually people no longer worried about the future because there were no people.

A happier ending might run like this: Those who saw the danger began to do more than talk about it. They began to study human behavior with methods that had first evolved in physics and biology. They turned from observing what people had done up to that time to observing what people did under carefully controlled conditions. A science and a technology of behavior emerged that were free of governmental, religious, and economic ideologies. Better cultural practices were designed. Meanwhile, older practices grew weak as their justifications became suspect. Governments no longer provided order and security. Religions failed to give peace of mind and joined with governments in threatening the peace of the world. Their answers to puzzling questions yielded to the answers of science. Economic institutions lost control as automation destroyed both the need for and the enjoyment of productive labor. Education emerged as the dominant force in the maintenance and transmission of cultural practices. The species survived for many thousands of years, and before those visitors from outer space reached Earth, they were met by a similar caravan coming from Earth itself.

Agreed, that is a utopian ending—but in which of the two senses of that word? Is it to be a better world, or no world at all?

chapter 2

What Is Wrong with Daily Life in the Western World?

ཀ፝ཀ፝ཀ፝ཀ፝ཀ፝ཀ፝ཀ፝ཀ

There are many things wrong with the world today, but they do not disturb everyone. Overpopulation, the impoverishment and pollution of the environment, and even the possibility of a nuclear war are often dismissed as matters of a fairly distant future. Poverty, illness, and violence are current problems, but not for everyone. Many of those who live in the Western democracies enjoy a reasonable degree of affluence, freedom, and security. But they have a problem of their own. In spite of their privileges, many are bored, listless, or depressed. They are not enjoying their lives. They do not like what they are doing; they are not doing what they like to do. In a word, they are unhappy. That is not the most serious problem in the world, but it could be said to be an ultimate one. Something like the current life style in the West is what most of the world look forward to as something to be enjoyed when they have solved the other problems. Is there not something more promising in the future of the species?

These are statements about how people feel. It is standard practice to phrase them that way. For centuries feelings have been accepted as both the causes and the effects of behavior. People are said to do what they do because they feel like doing it, and feel as they feel because of what they have done. Because feelings appear to play such an important role, it has been argued that a science of behavior must be incomplete, that it cannot solve the kind of problem we are concerned with here.

Feelings are not out of reach of a behavioral science, however. The question is not what feelings are, but what is felt. *Feel* is a verb—like *see, hear,* or *taste.* We see, hear, and taste things in the world around us, and we feel things in our bodies. When we feel lame, we are feeling lame muscles; when we feel tired, we are feeling a tired body; when we have a toothache, we are feeling an inflamed tooth. Feeling differs from other kinds of sensing in several ways. Because what we feel is within our skin, we cannot escape from it. The sense organs with which we feel it are not as easily observed as those with which we see things in the world around us. And we cannot report what we feel as accurately as what we see because those who teach us to do so lack information about the body we feel. We need not pursue these epistemological issues further, however, in order to state the present question: What do we feel when we are not enjoying our lives? And, of course, what must we change if we are to feel differently?

I suggest that answers are to be found in something that has happened in the history of the species. The first members of *Homo sapiens* must have been very much like the other primates we see today. They would have had their own ways of gathering or hunting for food, building shelters, finding mates, raising a family, and avoiding harm. Their behavior would have been as much the product of natural selection as that of other primates, and perhaps no more readily modified through conditioning. Like other species, they would have profited from the experience of others, but only through imitation and modeling.

The human species took a unique evolutionary step when its vocal musculature came under operant control and language was born. People could then tell as well as show each other what to do. Extraordinarily complex social environments, or cultures, evolved, and they gave the species its extraordinary power. I shall argue that, at the same time, many of the new cultural practices eroded or destroyed certain relations between organism and environment that prevailed when operant conditioning evolved.

The result is easily described as a matter of feelings because the feelings at issue are closely tied to operant reinforcement. Thus, we say that reinforcing things *please* us, that we *like* them, that they *feel good*. The association of reinforcement with feeling is so strong that it has long been said that things reinforce *because* they feel good or feel good *because* they reinforce. We should say, instead, that things both feel good *and* reinforce because of what has happened in the evolution of the species.

Organisms presumably eat nourishing foods because genetic variations that increased their likelihood of doing so contributed to the survival of the individual and the species and thus were selected. For simpler species, we do not often say that the foods must "taste good." The issue of enjoyment presumably arose when organisms became susceptible to reinforcement by the same foods. They then ate for two reasons: The behavior was innate and was also reinforced by its consequences. It is the reinforcing effect, not the genetic tendency to eat, that we report when we say that foods "taste good."

Reinforcement, however, has another effect: Behavior that is reinforced is more likely to occur again. At the risk of being seriously misunderstood by critics of behaviorism, I shall distinguish between the *pleasing* and the *strengthening* effects. They occur at different times and are felt as different things. When we feel pleased, we are not necessarily feeling a greater inclination to behave in the same way. (Indeed, when we call a reinforcer satisfying rather than pleasing, as Thorndike did, we suggest that it *reduces* the likelihood of acting in the same way, because *satisfying* is etymologically close to *satiating*.) When we repeat behavior that has been reinforced, on the other hand, we do not feel the pleasing effect we felt at the time the reinforcement occurred. *Pleasing* appears to be the everyday English word that is closest to *reinforcing,* but it covers only half the effect.

I am arguing that cultural practices have evolved primarily because of the pleasing effect of reinforcement, and that much of the strengthening effect of the consequences of behavior has been lost. The evolution of cultural practices has miscarried. It is rather like what has happened in the field of health. The species evolved in an environment with a given mean temperature and humidity, a given purity of water, given kinds of food, and given predators, including viruses and bacteria. Cultural practices have vastly changed all that, and because natural selection has been too slow to keep pace, we suffer many illnesses from which the species must once have been free. The world we live in is largely a creation of people, and nowhere more so than in the West—but in an important sense it is not well made.

Before looking more closely at what is wrong, it will be helpful to review five cultural practices that, by promoting the pleasing effects of the consequences of behavior at the expense of the strengthening effects, have eroded contingencies of reinforcement.

I begin with an old chestnut, the alienation of the worker from the product of his work. That is Karl Marx, of course, and it is often assumed that Marx meant the *deprivation* of the worker of the product of his work. A better word is *estrangement*. The behavior of the industrial worker is separated from the kind of immediate consequences that shapes and maintains the behavior of, say, a craftsman. Alienation can scarcely be exploitation because entrepreneurs are also estranged from the consequences of what they do, and so are the workers in socialist states.

The reinforcer in question is money, but love of money is only indirectly the root of alienation. Money is a conditioned reinforcer: It becomes reinforcing only when it is exchanged for goods or services. It is always one step away from the kind of reinforcing consequences to which the species originally became susceptible. It is also a generalized reinforcer: It is exchanged for many different things. If you assemble a television set for your own use, you will not assemble another until you need one, but you exchange money for so many different things that you almost always need it. In a factory you assemble one set and then another.

The reinforcing effect of money is especially weak when it is paid on contract. The contingencies are aversive. Workers do not work "in order to be paid," if that means that the money they will receive at the end of the week affects their behavior during the week. They work to avoid being discharged and losing the money they would otherwise receive. Most of the time they do simply what they are told to do or have agreed to do. Having assembled part of a television set on a production line, the worker is not then more strongly inclined to assemble another. The contract must remain in force. Workers rarely put in a free day at the factory just because they have been paid for working there at other times.

Money is reinforcing when it is paid piece-rate or on commission (technically speaking, when behavior is reinforced on a fixed-ratio schedule), or when it is paid on the variable-ratio schedule of all gambling systems. Wages paid for the amount of time worked do not, strictly speaking, reinforce behavior at all.

(The strengthening effect is missed, by the way, when reinforcers are called rewards. *People* are rewarded, but *behavior* is reinforced. If, as you walk along the street, you look down and find some money, and if money is reinforcing, you will tend to look down again for some time. We should not say, however, that you were rewarded for looking down. As the history of the word shows, reward implies compensation, something that offsets a sacrifice or loss, if only the expenditure of effort. We give heroes medals, students degrees, and famous people prizes, but those rewards are not directly contingent upon what they have done, and it is generally felt that they would not be deserved if they had been worked for.)

Alienation of the worker is inevitable if the world is to profit from specialization and a division of labor. One person does not make a coat by raising sheep, shearing wool, spinning thread, weaving cloth, and making the cloth into a coat. Instead, one person raises sheep, another spins thread, and another weaves cloth, and each exchanges what he has done for a coat that still another person makes. There is no question of the gain from such specialization, but the inevitable consequence is that one person spends a greater amount of time doing only one kind of thing. Everyone knows what it means to be tired of doing too often the things one enjoys, and that is another reason why industries turn to essentially aversive measures to maintain the behavior of their workers.

In summary, industrial practices in Western cultures have made goods and services more readily available, but they have destroyed many of the natural contingencies of reinforcement.

A second source of erosion of the strengthening effect of reinforcement is closely related. As we have noted, most employers are as alienated from what is produced as are their employees. For thousands of years people have "saved labor" either by forcing slaves to work for them or by paying servants or employees. More recently, they have turned to labor-saving devices and robots. The aversive consequences of labor are saved, but the reinforcing ones are lost. Like the worker, the employer does fewer kinds of things and does each one more often. Consider the extent to which labor-saving devices have made us button pushers: We push buttons on elevators, telephones, dashboards, video recorders, washing machines, ovens, typewriters, and computers, all in exchange for actions that would at least have a bit of variety. Systems that save labor also save laborers, and the familiar problem of unemployment follows. But even if everyone could enjoy a share of the labor saved, there would still be alienation.

In some parts of America, people who work for others are called "the help," but help does not always have to be paid for. Benevolent cultures help small children, the handicapped, the ill, and the aged. Such cultures are less vulnerable to defection and more likely to solve their problems, but harmful consequences follow when they help those who can help themselves. Helping children do something they can do alone deprives them of reinforcing consequences that would shape and maintain more useful behavior. Helping older people to do things they could do for themselves deprives them of the opportunity to engage in reinforced activities.

In the Western democracies, people are also freer than elsewhere from other kinds of aversive conditions. The Atlantic Charter guarantees freedom from fear and freedom from want. Perhaps there is no part of the world in which everyone enjoys the right to security and access to goods, but the Western democracies have gone the farthest in that direction. In many ways they may have gone too far. What has happened resembles the illness called anorexia nervosa, in which an overweight person begins a program of weight reduction, reaches a satisfactory weight, and proceeds to become emaciated. Something of the sort has happened as we have moved toward a way of life that is free of all kinds of unpleasant things. We resist not only the constraints imposed by tyrannical governments and religions but also seat belts, hard hats, and no-smoking signs. We escape not only painful extremes of temperature and exhausting work but also the mildest discomforts and annoyances. As a result, there is very little left to escape or prevent. The strengthening consequences of negative reinforcement that we enjoy as relief have been lost. We are suffering from what might be called *libertas nervosa*.

Perhaps there is no part of the world in which no one goes hungry, needs medical care, or has no place to live, but Western cultures have gone the farthest in alleviating those hardships. To the extent that we care for our members beyond the point at which they could care for themselves, they are suffering from what might be called *caritas nervosa*.

In summary, people who avoid labor and have things done for them escape from many aversive consequences, but beyond a certain point they deprive themselves of strengthening consequences as well.

The strengthening effect of reinforcement is eroded in a third way when people do things only because they have been told to do them. They buy the car they are advised to buy; they see the movie they are told to see; they shop at the store they are told to shop at. In Western cultures there has been a great expansion of this "rule-governed" behavior.

Advice is important, of course. No one could acquire a very large repertoire of behavior during a single lifetime without it. Someone tells us what to do and what consequences will follow, and we do it and the consequences follow; the behavior then becomes part of our reinforced repertoire, and we forget the advice. Until consequences have followed, however, we take advice only because doing so has had reinforcing consequences, quite possibly of a different kind. We have done different things, and the consequences need not have been related to our present state of deprivation. If the friend who tells us that a particular restaurant serves excellent food has advised us in the past only about books that we have enjoyed reading, we shall be less inclined to go to the restaurant than if the friend had advised us about food, and still less inclined, of course, than if, advised or not, we had gone and found the food good.

We are also not strongly inclined to take advice if consequences have not often followed when we have done so. We may not always reach the point at which they follow. Formal education is largely a kind of advice, but little of the behavior shaped and maintained in the classroom is ever subsequently reinforced in daily life. The education is therefore advice that we are not strongly inclined to take. Consequences also do not follow when advice is bad. It is easy to understand why people so often resist doing what they are advised to do and resent, rather than thank, those who give advice.

The kind of advice called science is usually worth taking because it is more extensive than personal exposure to contingencies. But when we simply do what science tells us to do, the consequences are often long deferred. Some of them are only predicted and have not yet occurred to anyone. The gains are great, but a strengthening effect is often missing. Few people ever do only what science tells them to do.

Some of the advice we follow is the kind we give ourselves. We examine a set of contingencies and formulate a rule or plan. When we follow the rule or plan, we are said to act rationally, in the sense that we act for a reason we can name. But unless we are very good at analyzing contingencies, many of the consequences we predict will never occur. We are seldom as strongly inclined to behave rationally as we are inclined to act according to experienced consequences.

In summary, we take advice not because of the consequences that will follow in a given instance but because of consequences that have followed in the past. Most of the strength of our behavior is borrowed from the reinforcement of different behavior in different settings.

A fourth kind of cultural practice that reduces the strengthening effect of reinforcement also involves rules, but the rules are stronger. People tend to act in ways that please or avoid displeasing others, in part because the others respond in appropriate ways, but they are less inclined to behave well when they are merely observing rules of good conduct. Rules are extraordinarily important, of course, because they enable people to please or avoid displeasing others without submitting to possibly punitive consequences, and to respond in appropriate ways when pleased or displeased. As with advice, however, people observe rules because of the contingencies under which they learned to do so or because reinforcing consequences have followed when they observed other rules. They are less inclined to behave well than when face-to-face commendation or censure has followed.

Reinforcing consequences are further eroded when ethical rules are replaced by laws. The laws of governments and religions are maintained primarily for the sake of the institutions. Consequences such as security or peace of mind also follow for the individual (otherwise, the institutions would not have survived as cultural practices), but they are usually deferred. Moreover, cultural practices change faster than rules and laws, and people therefore often "do what is right" for reasons that are no longer advantageous to anyone. Contingencies of control maintained by governments and religions are at times so powerful that those who respond to them report the exaltation or ecstasy associated with escape from a severe threat of punishment. Others, though, have as strongly resisted such control.

In summary, then, when people behave well either by following ethical rules or by obeying the laws of a government or religion, personal strengthening consequences are usually long deferred.

A fifth source of the erosion of natural contingencies is different. Many of the practices of advanced cultures appear to *increase* the frequency of immediate reinforcement. The West is especially rich in the things we call interesting, beautiful, delicious, entertaining, and exciting. These things make daily life more reinforcing, but they reinforce little more than the behavior that brings one into contact with them. Beautiful pictures reinforce looking at them, delicious foods reinforce eating them, entertaining performances and exciting games reinforce watching them, and interesting books reinforce reading them—but nothing else is done. Although we look at a nude statue in part because a tendency to look at similar forms has played a part in the survival of the species, looking does not have that effect in this instance. We look at a painting by Cezanne but do not eat the apples. We listen to a piece of music by Smetana but do not swim in the Moldau. Reinforcing effects occur, but they are not contingent upon the kind of behavior with respect to which the susceptibilities to reinforcement evolved.

The excitement of gambling, like the enjoyment of interesting or beautiful things, is also something that occurs when nothing more is done. When we buy lottery tickets, play blackjack or poker, operate slot machines, or play roulette, we do a very small number of things a very large number of times. Every winning play has a pleasing effect, but it is scheduled in such a way that the ultimate consequences are almost always either zero or negative. (In the long run, gamblers must lose if gambling enterprises are to succeed.) We enjoy gambling, as we enjoy looking and listening, but only a very small sample of our behavior is strengthened.

It may not seem that one could fail to enjoy a life spent looking at beautiful things, eating delicious foods, watching entertaining performances, and playing roulette. But it would be a life in which almost nothing else was done, and few of those who have been able to try it have been notably happy. What is wrong with life in the West is not that it has too many reinforcers, but that the reinforcers are not contingent upon the kinds of behavior that sustain the individual or promote the survival of the culture or species.

In summary, Western cultures have created many opportunities to do things that have pleasing consequences, but they are not the things whose consequences became strengthening.

Here, then, are five kinds of cultural practices that have eroded the contingencies of reinforcement under which the process of operant conditioning must have evolved:

1. People work for wages, but most of what they produce does not directly reinforce their behavior. The group profits from a division of labor and from specialization, but workers are alienated from the product of their work. Employers must invoke aversive sanctions.

2. People pay others to produce the things they consume, and thus avoid the aversive side of work, but they lose the reinforcing side as well. So do those who are helped by others when they could help themselves.

3. People do many things simply on advice, but only because reinforcing consequences have followed when they have taken other kinds of advice. They avoid the cost of exploring new contingencies but miss the reinforcers that would have followed if they had not done so.

4. By observing rules and obeying laws, people avoid punishment, either by their acquaintances or by a government or religion. The personal consequences that "justify" the rules or laws are indirect and usually long deferred.

5. People look at beautiful things, listen to beautiful music, and watch exciting entertainments, but the only behaviors reinforced are looking, listening, and watching. When people gamble, they do a very few things a very large number of times, and eventually without gain.

We might put the result very generally in this way: Where thousands of millions of people in other parts of the world cannot do many of the things they want to do, hundreds of millions in the West do not want to do many of the things they can do. In winning the struggle for freedom and the pursuit of happiness, the West has lost its inclination to act.

A conclusion of that sort is too sweeping to be accurate, however, and it does not suggest a solution to our problem. A more detailed analysis is needed, and it must start a long way back. We think of the human species as the most advanced, but not, of course, in every way. It is not the swiftest or the strongest, nor are its senses the keenest. It is evidently the most skillful. Man was once *Homo habilis,* literally "handyman." He had unusual hands and made unusual things. Then he became *Homo sapiens,* but not in the sense of "sapient." *Sapiens* first meant discerning or, specifically, tasting. (We still say "good taste" when we mean nothing more than discernment.) Much more was to happen before man could claim sapience in another sense, and it happened not to man but to the world in which he lived.

When the vocal apparatus of *Homo sapiens* came under operant control, language was born and with it a much more rapid evolution of cultural practices. These practices brought extraordinary gains, which are seen most clearly in the affluence, health, pleasure, and freedom of the West, but the world was no longer the world in which the species evolved. Early man did not work for others or pay others to work for him. He did not act merely as advised to act (he could imitate others, but only in roughly the same setting). He did not observe rules or obey laws. He did not look at pictures or listen to music or gamble (life was a gamble, but the payoff was life itself). When he had nothing to do, if we may judge from related species, early man simply slept or did nothing.

It is easier to describe the contributions of cultural practices than to say what went wrong. To reinforce means quite simply to strengthen, and when the strengthening consequences of behavior were sacrificed for the sake of the pleasing ones, *behavior simply grew weak.* That is not a very impressive conclusion, and it is hard to make clear what it means. Strength is a basic concept in the analysis of operant behavior, but there is no good word for it in everyday English. Metaphors are never quite apt. Some of them appeal to combustion. Active people are called *ardent* or *fervent*, words that once meant burning and boiling, respectively. (We still say a person is hot or cold, and not only with respect to sex.) Some metaphors allude to causes: *Zealous* once meant driven. Many refer to personal commitments: people are dedicated, devoted, or *engagés*. But there seems to be no word, metaphorical or otherwise, for strength itself.

It is possible that a word is lacking because behavior is often regarded as a mere sign or symptom. The important things are said to happen in an inner world of feelings and states of mind. There we do find terms that refer to strength or its lack. For example, the West is said to be suffering from a failure of will (call it abulia), a lack of compassion (call it apathy), a weakness of nerve (call it neurasthenia), or a weak libido (call it a weak libido). We use terms of that sort easily and with great satisfaction even though no one has ever adequately explained what they mean. The effect is to direct attention away from the environmental conditions that would be more helpful in explaining and changing behavior.

As an established scientific term, *strength* refers to the probability that an organism will behave in a given way at a given time. *Probability* is hard to define and measure, but rate of response is a sensitive dependent variable that is related. In the laboratory we watch the strength of a behavior change as we change the variables of which it is a function. When for the first time we make a reinforcer contingent upon a response, we bring an operant into existence. When we withdraw the reinforcer, we watch the behavior become extinct. We maintain steady levels of strength over a wide range of values with various schedules of reinforcement.

The cultural practices we have examined weaken behavior in a special way. They change the temporal relation between behavior and its consequences, especially through the use of conditioned and generalized reinforcers. The effect can be corrected by restoring more strengthening contingencies. Once we understand that, our problem may be simpler than we think. It is much easier to change contingencies of reinforcement than to restore will, refill a reservoir of psychic energy, or strengthen nerves. Contingencies of reinforcement are an important topic in the experimental analysis of behavior, and what is wrong with daily life in the West is precisely the field of *applied behavior analysis*. That term is better than *behavior modification* because it does not mean prescribing drugs, implanting electrodes, or performing surgery. It means improving the strengthening contingencies of behavior. Three familiar fields in which applied behavior analysis is doing this are education, behavior therapy, and industrial counseling.

The task of education is to build a repertoire of behavior that will eventually have reinforcing consequences in the daily and professional life of the graduate. Meanwhile, teachers provide temporary instructional contingencies, some of them social. The teacher is part of the world of the student, either as a model or as an arranger of reinforcing consequences. Historically the consequences have been almost always punitive: if not the birch rod or cane, then criticism or failure. The three classical by-products of punishment follow: escape (truancy), counterattack (vandalism), and stubborn inaction. Efforts to use the natural reinforcers of daily life have sacrificed the famous basics of reading, writing, and arithmetic, for which there are no natural reinforcers. The student who can read comes into contact with the reinforcers that writers put into what they write, but those reinforcers are out of reach until that student learns to read with some fluency. Meanwhile, contrived reinforcers can be used, but teachers who understand classroom management and the proper construction of programmed materials can use the unconditioned reinforcers of success and signs of progress. The repertoires they construct will have both pleasing and strengthening consequences when teaching ends.

Much the same thing can be said of operant therapy. Therapy using respondent, or Pavlovian, conditioning is different. Desensitization, for example, works either by extinguishing conditioned reflexes or permitting disturbing "instinctive" responses to "adapt out." There may be a strengthening effect if operant behavior has been suppressed, but operant therapy is directly a matter of strengthening. The counselor, like the teacher, is a temporary part of a social environment. Aversive measures were once common in counseling, but counselors now turn to them much less often than do teachers. As in teaching, the behavior they strengthen must have reinforcing consequences not only in the presence of the counselor but later in the world at large.

Many people spend a large part of their time at work. Especially since the Industrial Revolution, the pattern has been, as in education, "work or suffer the consequences"—in this case, discharge and the loss of a scheduled wage. The same standard effects of aversive control are evident: escape (absenteeism), counterattack (sabotage), and as little action as possible. Classical remedies, such as letting the worker have a greater share in decision making, do not attack the central problem, which lies in the contingencies, where changes are beginning to be made.

Progress is not as clear in other fields. Only a few of those who control the governmental and religious sanctions of daily life understand the problem or what can be done to solve it. The contingencies are there, however, and they will presumably be improved as soon as their role is understood.

Proposals to build a better world are usually rejected either as hopelessly utopian or as threats to the status quo. Governments naturally resist defection and revolution; religions resist apostasy and reformation; and industries resist nationalization and the control of prices and wages. There seems to be no reason, however, for anyone to resist the kind of change needed here. Citizens, communicants, and employees will contribute as much to their respective agencies when aversive consequences have been replaced by alternatives that please and strengthen.

That cultures have often turned to punitive control may be the best evidence we have that they have neglected strengthening alternatives. A reduction in punitive control would improve life in still another way. When people work only to avoid losing a job, study only to avoid failure, and treat each other well only to avoid censure or institutional punishment, the threatening contingencies generalize. It always seems as if there must be something that one ought to be doing. As a result, very few people can simply do nothing. They can relax only with the help of sedatives or tranquilizers, or by deliberately *practicing* relaxation. They can sleep only with the help of sleeping pills, of which billions are sold in the West every year. They are puzzled by, and envy, those in less developed countries whom they see happily doing nothing.

The quality of life in the West is not the most important problem in the world today. It cannot compare with global poverty, illness, and violence, or with overpopulation, the exhaustion of critical resources, the destruction of the environment, or the possibility of a nuclear war. But a better quality of life should help to solve those problems. Since the West is taken as a model by the rest of the world, it would be a more challenging model if it were improved. It would also be easier to copy. Other cultures would not need to make our mistakes.

And, after all, how much pollution and overconsumption would be avoided if the West, which is by far the greater offender, were to end its frantic search for enjoyable things to do? How much richer would the whole world be if the reinforcers in daily life were more effectively contingent on productive work? Above all, how many of the wars of history have been fought—how many could be fought—only because people did not enjoy their lives?

In one way or another much of this has been said before. Certainly this is not the first time that anyone has pointed to the damaging side effects of civilization. That was a central theme of the Enlightenment. "Man," said Rousseau, "is born free and he is everywhere in chains," but that is only one instance. And certainly this is not the first time anyone has asked, What is the good life? or, How can it be achieved? But there may be something new in the present answer. Traditional answers have taken many lines. Epicureans have sought the good life through multiplying their pleasures. Stoics have tried to live "above pleasure and pain." Many have looked for answers in a *vita monastica* or a strict puritanism. Eastern mystics have claimed to "abolish boredom by cherishing happiness." Rationalists have turned to skillful self-management. All such solutions began as personal experiences. They have served as cultural variations to be tested by their effect on the survival of the practicing group. None has been successful beyond the establishment of a fragmentary culture.

A solution based on scientific principles may have a better chance. We are beginning to see why people act as they do, and the reasons are of a sort that can be changed. A new set of practices cannot simply be imposed by a government, religion, or economic system; if it were, it would not be the right set of practices. It must play its part only as a variation to be tested by its survival value. The contingencies of selection are beyond our control. Cultures evolve much faster than species, but the kind of change that we need will still take a long time. We must be prepared to wait.

Perhaps it is reassuring that what is wrong with daily life, apart from all the other things that are wrong with the world, is a problem most characteristic of the West. It is perhaps reassuring because the West has also supported science, particularly behavioral science, most actively. It is therefore a setting in which the problem and a possible solution have come together for the first time.

chapter 3

News from Nowhere, 1984

❦❧❦❧❦❧❦❧❦❧

My title may have led you to think that I am going to talk about books. News from Nowhere *is a nineteenth-century utopia written by William Morris, the inventor of the Morris chair, an example of which graced every college dormitory room in my day. A comment would be appropriate because this is a centennial. Just one hundred years ago, Morris founded the Socialist League. It was socialism with a fairly small* s, *the utopian socialism of St. Simon, Fourier, and Robert Owen. Seven years later he pictured an idyllic life under socialism in his book. The other book you may have expected me to talk about is, of course,* Nineteen Eighty-four, *the twentieth-century dystopia by George Orwell. It describes what can happen to socialism no matter how well intentioned its origin. It is not very much like* News from Nowhere. *But I am not going to talk about books. My title simply means that in this year of 1984 I bring you news from a different nowhere, or rather I have asked an old friend to do so.*

My name is Burris. I live in an experimental community called Walden Two. In 1948 I published an account of how I discovered that community and came to join it. I have been living there ever since. I am told you may be interested in hearing about what has happened there and in particular about a man who joined the community in 1950.

I had noticed a newcomer to Walden Two, in part because he seemed to be noticing me. He was tall and thin and growing a beard that was still at a rather moth-eaten stage. One morning as I was having breakfast he brought his tray to my table and said, "May I?"

"Yes, of course," I said, and he put the tray down.

"I'm going back for a cup of coffee. May I take your cup and top it up?" I said that would be very kind of him.

He brought the cups back to the table, sat down, and held out his hand.

"My name is Blair," he said. "You are Burris?" I said I was. "You are the official historian of Walden Two—am I right?"

"Well, not official. Mr. Frazier doesn't think much of history."

"But unofficially," he said, "you must keep some kind of record." I admitted that I did. "Good. That's enough. I am hoping to join Walden Two. I have an appointment with the Admissions Committee this morning. I'll tell them most of what they want to know, but there is one thing I prefer to keep to myself. Yet I feel it ought to be on the record. May I ask you to keep a confidence?" I said I saw no reason why I should not. "Good. The fact is that in order to join Walden Two I have had to kill a man."

"Oh, wait!" I said angrily. "That's not fair. I'm not a therapist or priest—you had no right to ask me to keep that kind of confidence."

He laughed. "It's not quite the way it sounds." He drew out his wallet and started to take something from it. But then, holding one corner of the wallet by thumb and forefinger, he let it fall open. It looked a little like the skin of a small animal. "I shall enjoy throwing *that* away," he said. Then he took a clipping from the wallet and handed it to me. On it he had written *"Times*, London, January 22, 1950." It began: "DEATH OF GEORGE ORWELL. Eric Arthur Blair, better known to millions as George Orwell, the author of *Animal Farm* and *Nineteen Eighty-four*, died yesterday of tuberculosis . . . ."

I stared at the man across the table. *"You* are George Orwell?"

"No!" he said, laughing. "I *was*. But, you see" (he pointed to the clipping), "I've killed him. A body was found missing from another ward in the hospital. I had left. I learned that kind of trick in the Spanish War."

"You faked your death? But why?"

"Orwell was an unhappy man. A bitter man. Have you read 'Such Were the Joys'—about his frightful schooling? Have you read *Down and Out in Paris* or *Keep the Aspidistra Flying*—how awful it was to be poor? Have you read *Animal Farm* or *Nineteen Eighty-four*—the specter of the totalitarian state? He had no hope. No reason to live."

"And so you killed him. But why come here?"

"I read your book, and I saw something that I thought you and Frazier had missed. I came to tell you how to do a better job, but I like what I see and I've decided to stay, if you'll take me. I was looking for a chance to live a *happy* life, and I may have found it. So here I am. And now I have another favor to ask." I looked at him, a bit worried. "Take me to your leader."

The old cliché disturbed me. He meant Frazier, of course. Frazier had founded Walden Two and was still living there, but he was far from a leader. He had concealed his part in Walden Two as far as possible. He not only disliked history; he buried it. He was no longer a Planner. Anyone less like a leader would be hard to find.

Of course I took Blair to meet Frazier, and the discussions that followed covered a period of more than twenty-five years. Somehow I managed to be present at most of them and took notes. At first I would hurry back to my room to put down all I could remember, but eventually I carried a notebook.

Later, when pocket recorders were available, I often used one. I think I can guarantee the accuracy of what follows.

What had impressed Blair and brought him to Walden Two was the lack of any institutionalized government, religion, or economic system. That had been the dream of nineteeth-century anarchism, but it had gone wrong. Evidently it had gone right in Walden Two.

"You are the perfect anarchist," Blair said to Frazier one day.

"I'll agree," said Frazier, "if you don't mean a man with a bomb. People have never liked their governments for very long and have changed them, but they have only put other governments in their place. It wasn't until the nineteenth century that anyone seriously proposed that governments simply be disbanded. How to disband them was the problem.

"The early anarchists wanted a peaceful change. I think you can say that for Marx. Arrange for a just distribution of the proceeds, and voluntary agreement can replace authority. A temporary dictatorship may be needed, but it will wither away. But then the terrorists took over. Destroy the present government whether or not you have anything to put in its place. Anarchy no longer meant the absence of government; it meant disorder, chaos."

"But not in Walden Two," said Blair. "What's the secret?"

"You simply turn from one kind of law to another."

"I'm afraid you'll have to explain that," said Blair.

"Human behavior is selected by its consequences. At first it must have been selected by the physical environment, but later people could talk about consequences. They could give advice and warn each other of danger. They could avoid exposure to the consequences by taking the advice of those who had been exposed to them. Eventually they formulated rules of action, and that led to the laws of science. It was Francis Bacon who pointed to a similarity with the laws of government, but he missed an important difference.

"The laws of governments and religions are useful. They tell members of a group how to avoid punishment (without being punished), and they tell the group how to punish consistently. The great codifiers of social practices have been justly honored. It was the administration of laws that caused trouble. Those who found themselves in possession of administrative power could never resist using it to their own aggrandizement. To justify themselves, they invented myths—like the divine right of kings, priests, or possessors of wealth. The effect was wholesale exploitation.

"In the nineteenth century something else began to be understood. The problem was not only exploitation. People were behaving more and more by following rules and less and less because of the natural consequences of their behavior. It was Max Weber who pointed to the bureaucratization needed to enforce rules and Marx who emphasized the alienation of the worker from the natural consequences of his work.

"At the start of his career, Marx got it right. The working classes were suffering more from alienation than from exploitation, as bad as that may have been. Of course Marx put it all in terms of feelings (he was not a full-fledged behaviorist, alas), but it is easy enough to put it right. It all comes down to consequences—to contingencies of reinforcement. Workers who are said to feel *powerless* have nothing to show for their work but their wages, nothing that is theirs that they have done. Workers who are said to feel *estranged* from society are spending too much of their day untouched by social contingencies. What it means to say that a worker is *depersonalized* is a little harder to explain. A person or self is a repertoire of behavior. The repertoire shaped and maintained by daily life is rich and varied. The repertoire shaped and maintained by a factory is small and stale. It does not compose much of a person.

"Marx made all that clear but dropped it when he began to emphasize exploitation. Exploitation was a better ground to fight on. It is not hard to persuade workers that they are underpaid. It is harder to rouse them to action because they feel estranged, powerless, or depersonalized. The issue of exploitation could also be dramatized—as a struggle between capitalist and worker, between bourgeoisie and proletariat.

"Ironically, the socialistic or communistic systems that corrected for exploitation with a more equitable distribution of the proceeds left alienation unchanged. The proletariat in a communist country may share the wealth, but the on-the-job contingencies are no better than in capitalist countries and probably worse. They breed just as much alienation. Walden Two is state ownership without a state. Its members are not employed, because there is no employer. They come into direct contact with the world as people did before there were governments, religions, or industries. They have immediate reasons for behaving—and they behave in ways that not only support their way of life but give them the sense of satisfaction that comes from effective action."

"Marx took off from Hegel," said Blair, "but for Hegel alienation was something that went on inside a person. That doesn't seem to make sense."

"It makes perfectly good sense," said Frazier with his usual bluntness. "When people began to talk about their behavior one person could ask another, 'What are you doing?' 'Why are you doing that?' 'How do you feel?' Those verbal contingencies gave rise to consciousness, or self-knowledge. Hegel said that alienation followed when 'consciousness divided itself into subject and object.' A behaviorist would say that alienation follows when a person is divided into two selves—an observer and an observed. Psychiatrists use the word alienation in more or less that way. All behavior is unconscious—the product of contingencies of reinforcement. We share unconscious behavior with the other animals. Behavior becomes conscious when society gives us reasons to examine ourselves. There is also a division between controlling and controlled selves. Behavior shaped and maintained by its immediate consequences is not only unconscious, it is unrational, unreasoned, unplanned. Social contingencies breed self-management. We make our own rules and follow them. Those are extraordinary gains, but they nevertheless alienate us from immediate contact with the great genetic reinforcers or the conditioned reinforcers based on them."

"That still doesn't sound like Marx's alienation," said Blair.

"Marx was talking about a special set of cultural practices, a special set of reasons for behaving—namely, wages. They defer the natural reinforcing consequences of craftsmanship, if they do not destroy them."

In the 1960s Frazier and Blair watched another version of anarchism—the so-called hippie movement. Young people turned against government. They broke laws, trashed, and called the police *pigs* ("'Make love, not war' was almost right," said Frazier. "But it should have been 'Make love, not laws.'") They turned from the religion of their families to uninstitutionalized Eastern mysticism. They turned against industry, begging or living on checks from home. Like the nineteenth-century anarchists, they proposed to destroy the present system before deciding what to put in its place. To Frazier's irritation, they formed communities of a sort. They had their gurus: Norman O. Brown with his Freudian permissiveness and Herbert Marcuse with his mixture of Freud and Marx. Frazier may have been jealous, but when I told him that sales of *Walden Two* were soaring, he was annoyed. "There is no connection whatsoever," he insisted.

Blair contended that there were vestiges of government in Walden Two. "Maybe it's the *world* of Walden Two that controls its citizens and not a government, religion, or industry, but it nevertheless controls," he said. "And control for the good of everyone is still control. Where do you find personal freedom or a sense of personal worth or dignity?"

"Freedom and dignity are feelings," replied Frazier. "They are collateral products of contingencies of reinforcement. Under negative reinforcement we do what we *have* to do, and we don't feel free. We may not feel free under positive reinforcement, either, if it is so powerful that it keeps us from doing things we should like to do. Slaves obviously do not feel free, but workers do not feel free either if they must work so long and hard that they have no time or energy for anything else. In Walden Two we behave under relatively undemanding contingencies of positive reinforcement, and we feel free.

"And we also get credit. The contingencies may be maintained by the community, and a behavioral engineer may have designed them and changed them from time to time in the light of experience, but the consequences are nonetheless directly reinforcing. There is no alienating intermediary; hence, we enjoy a strong feeling of personal dignity or worth."

Frazier had a curious contempt for labor-saving devices. "Naturally we avoid exhausting or dangerous work if we can," he said, "but we go too far. There is something in operant conditioning that is important to health and happiness even when the consequences are not very reinforcing or even slightly aversive."

"But it's human nature to avoid work," said Blair.

"And if it is, we know why," said Frazier. "Escape from unnecessary work must once have had great survival value. When you must spend all day hunting or gathering, there is a point in saving energy when you can. The mistake is to save it all. Slaves were early labor-saving devices but difficult to keep in good working order. Servants replaced them but proved too costly for most people. Now we have machines and robots. They are costly too, and often unreliable, but technology has brought them within reach of many of us. We no longer wash dishes, but use a dishwasher."

"You *enjoy* washing dishes?"

"Perhaps I don't enjoy it, but I get something out of it that I lose when I put dishes in a dishwasher. It's what Carlyle meant when he said that all work is noble, even cotton spinning."

"Surely you are not going to defend the mills of nineteenth-century England," said Blair. "There was nothing noble about tending a spinning machine or loom fourteen hours a day."

"It was the fourteen hours that was wrong," said Frazier. "Many women enjoy knitting, and I am sure I would too if our culture permitted. Many people own looms and work on them with pleasure. There is something about washing and drying a dish that is missing when you put it in a dishwasher. Wash it by hand, and you see it come clean. You have *done* something. You have had an effect."

"You couldn't have told that to George Orwell," said Blair. "He knew what it meant to be a *plongeur* in a French restaurant."

"But now you are talking about quantities again. I'm talking about washing a *few* dishes. A few cherries are reinforcing, but if you must eat a bushel you will find the last quart hard work."

"But labor-saving devices let people do more important things."

"How many of them do? Those who use labor-saving devices—whether slaves, servants, or machines according to the century—we call the leisure class. What has it got to show for itself by way of better things?"

"Only all the literature, art, and music in the world," said Blair, with some satisfaction. "It has released writers, artists, and composers from less productive labor."

"But the writers, artists, and composers were not at leisure. You have identified the kinds of things that may justly replace the labor of everyday life, and if you will agree that labor-saving devices are to be used only if the labor saved is put to such uses, I'm with you. But what have the leisure classes actually done? They have turned to the variable-ratio schedules of gambling systems to give them something to do; they have sought an *ersatz* sense of achievement in alcohol and drugs; and they have overconsumed the basic genetic reinforcers of food, sex, and violence. And what is more ridiculous than the way they try to replace the labor they have saved and find the sense of achievement they have lost? Instead of washing a dish, they do exercises. Instead of spinning, they jog."

"I'm afraid I'd still like to be a member of the leisure class," said Blair. "But come to think of it, I *am*. Aren't the members of Walden Two a leisure class? Only four hours of work a day on the average! Weren't you thinking of saving labor when you designed the community?"

Frazier was always annoyed when anyone mentioned his role in founding Walden Two. "Walden Two," he said rather harshly, "is an environment in which people just naturally do the things they need to do to maintain themselves (with something to spare for the future) and treat each other well, and then just naturally do a hundred other things they enjoy doing because they do not *have* to do them. And when I say natural," he added hurriedly, "I simply mean positively reinforced. The labor we save in Walden Two is the unnecessary labor forced upon people by a badly designed environment."

Frazier was concerned about another way in which people were alienated from the reinforcing consequences of their behavior. "Welfare is a form of leisure," he said, "and it raises the same problems. Helping those who cannot help themselves strengthens a culture, but helping those who can help themselves destroys it. Everyone agrees that people on welfare would be better off if they were working. That is often a complaint about exploitation—the exploitation of the taxpayer—but the real harm is done to the recipient. Welfare payments are not effectively contingent on behavior. The health-giving side of operant reinforcement is missing. The helping professions have been slow to learn that lesson. Nursing homes find it easier to do things for old people than to let them do things for themselves, and by destroying the all-important contingencies of reinforcement, they make old people sick and miserable. At the heart of doing *anything* is something worth keeping."

The schools in Walden Two were no longer as I had described them. Teaching machines had come into use—at first rather crude mechanical devices, but then computers. Blair resisted the change at every step.

"You are violating your own principles," he said. "Could anything be more contrived and artificial than the reinforcement of operating a machine? You've returned to the factory. Students should be free to discover things for themselves."

"The greatest mistake you can make in designing education," said Frazier, "is to listen to John Dewey and the cognitive psychologists who have taken him up and talk about discovery. Of course we learn by discovery. Everything the species knows was discovered by somebody. But no one of us can discover more than the minutest fraction of human knowledge. The rest of what we know we must uncover. It is there to be learned and should be learned as easily and quickly as possible.

"With the evolution of verbal behavior, instruction could take the place of direct contact with the world. The real contingencies take over after instruction has occurred. Meanwhile something else is needed. For centuries that something was punishment. The student learned—or else! Programmed instruction turned to the genuine mediating reinforcers of success and progress. A good program first induces students to engage in behavior. The behavior is said to be *primed*. For a time, if fractional help is needed, the behavior is *prompted*. Prompts are then carefully removed, or *vanished*. What is left is behavior on its own! Q.E.D." He looked straight at Blair. "Quod erat demonstrandum," he said, and then, as if explaining, "Which was to be demonstrated."

I was embarrassed. Blair had had a classical education, and from time to time dropped a Latin phrase or two. He did not need help. Latin was not one of Frazier's strong points. He was showing off. Blair capped it nicely. "I'd prefer Q.E.I.," he said. "Quod erat inveniendum—Which was to be *discovered*."

Frazier moved quickly to another point. "The difference between programmed education and the *factory*," he said, "is the difference between a system that must withdraw its reinforcers before it can claim success and one that must maintain its contingencies forever. Government, religion, and capital can never relax. They not only shape new behavior, they must keep the contingencies in force. Education and counseling shape behavior, but they dismantle the contingencies as soon as the behavior is taken over by daily life.

"When Burris first came here, he saw some of our children driving pegs into the ground and running strings from one peg to another. As Burris put it, Euclid was getting a firsthand experimental check. (Wasn't it Gauss who did something like that, triangulating points on three hilltops to see if the angles in a triangle *really* added up to 180 degrees?) That is all very fine, but it won't get you very far into Euclid. A good program will take the average ten- or twelve-year-old through Euclid's *Elements* in a breeze. Burris was impressed by one of our temporary divagations."

One day Frazier was having tea with a child when Blair came up waving a magazine.

"Look at this," he said. "Somebody is giving us some help."

He would not have broken in so impolitely if Frazier had been talking with an older person, and Frazier was annoyed. He turned back to the child.

"Pulchrum in parvo," Blair said, insisting upon Frazier's attention.

Frazier was doubly annoyed. Latin again. He took the magazine, glanced at it, and handed it back. "Or, as the rest of us would say, 'Small is beautiful.'"

"Right," said Blair. "You must read it." It was a review of Schumacher's little book on the advantages of systems of moderate size, and the so-called intermediate technologies he was inventing for use in the Third World. I happened to be with Blair when Frazier met us the next day.

"Communities," Frazier said, speaking very carefully, "have always been *multum* in parvo, if not *pulchrum*." (I suspect he had been looking in a Latin dictionary.) "They are *miniature* states. They must be small if they are to be experimental. Where else is one to start who is not the head of a government, religion, or industry? Where has any science started, or any art or music? The trick is to *stay* small. Walden Two works because it *is* small. Cities need police forces just because they are big, because face-to-face control of decent personal behavior is impossible. Why be nice to anyone in a big city? Why not do shabby work if your next job will come from an ad in the Yellow Pages? Nothing but an organized punitive system will replace face-to-face censure and criticism, and nothing at all can replace commendation and gratitude."

Frazier began to talk about the Scandinavian countries. Sweden in particular had achieved an almost perfect socialism. Income taxes were about fifty percent, but no one seemed to mind. In return, education was free, from kindergarten through graduate school. There was free health care for everyone, and special housing for the elderly. In short, just about everything anyone needed. But something was wrong.

"It is the acme of rule-governed social behavior," Frazier said. "Those who pay their income tax can look at the happy schoolchild, the industrious college student, the comfortable aging couple, and say, 'We're helping them,' but they will never hear *them* say thank you. They are alienated from the product of their *social* behavior. They do nothing that has any immediate social consequences.

"The chances are that the contingencies in their work are also contrived. No one will ever correct the alienation of workers from the product of their labor in a large factory, no matter who owns the factory. Like the communist countries, Sweden has not made the 'social good' a strong reinforcer. You have to *see* a good, hold it in your hand, as citizens of Walden Two do so many times a day."

The library sent for Schumacher's book, and Frazier was as enthusiastic as Blair, not because only intermediate technologies would help developing countries but because nothing else would keep the production of goods a reinforcing consequence for the worker.

Small was also beautiful, Frazier pointed out, in the study of behavior. A laboratory setting was a small sample of daily life. Philosophers and psychologists had begun with massive samples. A few, like William James and Freud, had some success, but only because they were lucky. Happy accidents had given them glimpses of order. You could not expect to get very far that way. "Small animals in small spaces," Frazier exclaimed, patting Schumacher's book, "and beauty is truth, truth beauty." Blair knew nothing about the research Frazier was talking about, and as a matter of fact never learned about it.

Frazier himself had no qualms about inferring general principles from large things. "In the world as a whole," he said one day, "small may or may not be beautiful, but big is certainly ugly. We are getting on toward a population of five billion people. What can you do about that?"

"You certainly weren't doing very much," said Blair, "when your young women were having babies before they were twenty. You were adding an extra generation every hundred years. I remember how shocked I was when I read Burris's book."

"Burris was wrong, of course," said Frazier. "We were already changing. It is all very well to say that those who are intelligent enough to control their numbers should not do so because more intelligent people are needed, but if we are to design a way of life that will solve the problems of the world at large, it must be a way that stabilizes the population. Even when we were breeding too soon, Walden Two was eliminating all the spurious reasons for having children—the social pressures, the need for children as helpers in the family, accidental conception . . . and giving everyone who loves children a chance to be with them without breeding them."

"Small is not so beautiful," Blair said another time, "when it means sameness. Too much of the same thing, too many of the same faces. I like to travel. If I had not traveled fairly widely, would I be as happy as I am now?"

"You say you like to travel. Travel agencies and airlines should be sued for false claims. Who ever sees what their putative customers see in the advertisements? Of course there are still some beautiful cities, with beautiful buildings and museums, but it is no great sacrifice to learn about them from films or books. And anyway all that is beautiful in the world is being destroyed by your travelers—the natural beauty of our parklands, ancient buildings eaten away by the fumes of buses. How much better it would be if we spent our time and money on making our own world beautiful. And when I say beautiful, all I mean is that it will be the kind of place you go to and stay in just because it reinforces going to and staying there. Our fossil fuels would last hundreds of years longer if people stopped moving about."

Frazier was launched on a favorite theme. "Walden Two has solved most of the other problems facing the world today," he said. "We consume only as much as we need to maintain a friendly, productive, enjoyable life. We waste nothing; everything is recycled. We dress for the weather, allowing the weather indoors to range widely. We scarcely pollute the environment at all. We avoid hazardous wastes. We do it all and still enjoy our lives. Somehow or other the whole world must learn that secret or we are lost."

"But isn't the whole world going to be a different problem?" said Blair. "How long will it let you alone? You're hurting too many powerful people. Eventually you'll be attacked."

"And so we start building nuclear weapons? I grant you we can't do that. That is not an *intermediate* technology."

"I don't want to build weapons either," said Blair. "But what can you do to stop others from building them?"

"Not much, I'll admit. But it would be helpful to find out why they build them. That means finding out why they consume irreplaceable resources at such a fantastic rate, why they allow themselves to make the world nearly unlivable. Find that out and you will know why, in one last desperate struggle for a decent place to live and something to live with, they will turn to the ultimate horror of a nuclear war."

That was not enough for Blair. He could not see how Frazier's ideology, as he insisted on calling it, could remedy matters. In the 1970s he became quite feeble and perhaps for that reason more pessimistic. He gave up his room and moved to special quarters for those who needed care. When Frazier and I visited him there one day, we found him sitting up in bed. He surprised us by talking about George Orwell. He had mentioned him occasionally, and always, of course, as if he were another person, but now he seemed to be pulling himself together.

"When Orwell wrote *Nineteen Eighty-four*," he said, "he thought that sooner or later the world would be pretty much as he described it. He could not see any hope. It was all too obvious. Put government, religion, and capital together and you have the monstrous state, controlling practically all of what you behaviorists call the reinforcers. Of course it will use them for its own aggrandizement. It has no reason to do otherwise, and that is that.

"I came to Walden Two looking for something else, but have I found it? You have taught me too much about human behavior. Human nature, you say, is out of date. It's the product of a world that in many ways was much more immediately threatening than it is today. In that less hospitable world, for example, organisms evolved in such a way that they ate as much as possible whenever they could, especially salt and sugar, which were then in very short supply. And just because that became human nature, we now produce and eat far more than we need, especially the salty and sweet things that taste so good, and we ruin our health and are slowly exhausting the arable land of the world.

"And when from time to time famine and pestilence decimated the population, it was important that our species, like other species, breed as often as possible. To make sure that that would happen, sexual contact became highly reinforcing, as you put it. And now, as a result, we are filling up the world at a fantastic rate.

"In a precarious world, too, those who survived and reproduced their kind were those who fought well, and they fought best if signs of the damage they inflicted reinforced successful blows. Signs of damage became powerful reinforcers, and now a massive aggression threatens the world. And that's a threat for which evolution could not prepare us.

"The very human nature that once barely led to our survival will soon end our survival once and for all. Do you know that sonnet of Shakespeare's that begins, 'That time of year thou mayst in me behold'? It is an old man speaking to his young lover, but it could as well be the earth speaking to us all—

> That time of year thou mayst in me behold
> When yellow leaves, or none, or few, do hang
> Upon those boughs which shake against the cold,
> Bare ruined choirs, where late the sweet birds sang.
> In me thou seest the twilight of such day
> As after sunset fadeth in the west
> Which by and by black night doth take away,
> Death's second self, that seals up all in rest.
> In me thou seest the glowing of such fire
> That on the ashes of his youth doth lie,
> As the deathbed whereon it must expire,
> Consum'd with that which it was nourish'd by.

Blair paused. " 'Consum'd with that which it was nourished by.' Could you say it better? We are to be destroyed by the fabulous genetic endowment that has been the glory of the species. And what a different reading you can give the last two lines of that sonnet:

> This thou perceiv'st, which makes thy love more strong.
> To love that well, which thou must leave ere long.

We see that we are about to perish and we love life all the more—a life that our stronger loving will all the sooner bring to an end." With that, Blair turned his face to the wall, and Frazier and I quietly left.

Once outside, Frazier said, "Always the man of letters! He lacks the scientific spirit. Love of life! Doesn't he see that he is still talking about our genetic susceptibilities to rein-forcement? Maybe we can't *change* them, but we can build a world in which they will cause far less trouble." He groaned quietly and threw up his arms in a mock gesture of despair. I knew the sign. He was about to say something he had said a thousand times, something of which he was utterly convinced, yet something he had to say again and again because it was so little understood. I switched on my pocket recorder.

As Frazier so often did, he came to the point from an unexpected direction. "There is a spider that uses its silk to make, not a web, but a net. The spider hangs just above the ground, stretching the net with its legs. When an unsuspect-ing insect passes underneath, the spider wraps it in the net with lightning speed. It eats the insect and the net, recycling the silk. We must assume that that is all a product of natural selection, but it could not have occurred in its present form as a variation. It is the result of a long series of variations and contingencies of survival in which simpler versions gradually became more complex.

"The spider can be caught in a net too—a net made by a member of a different species, with behavior acquired through a different process of selection, operant conditioning. But in a single lifetime no one person could make a net without help. Too many variations would have to occur and be selected by their reinforcing consequences. Instead, netmaking evolved as a cultural practice, in a third kind of selection. Just as operant conditioning takes us beyond the range of behavior due to natural selection, so the evolution of cultural practices takes us beyond operant conditioning.

"The point is that netmaking did not simply evolve through the accumulation of lucky variations. Instead, people talked about nets, how they were made, and why they worked and how they could be made to work better. Cultural practices evolve, but they are also designed. Can anyone doubt that when a science of behavior tells us how to design better practices—and I don't mean better nations, religions, or business enterprises—we can deal with human nature adequately?"

"But I think what was bothering Blair," I said, "is whether there is time. Can we create a culture that has the chance of a future before our present cultures destroy us?"

Frazier stopped. He seemed to be trying to remember something he had intended to say, as if I had interrupted him. Then he said quickly, "I think there's time," and started to walk on.

I laid my hand on his arm and stopped him. "Do you *really* believe that?" I said. He pulled his arm free and walked on.

We did not see Blair again. He died the next day. His death was announced to the community, and Frazier and I, as his closest friends, scattered his ashes in one of the orchards. I had kept Blair's secret, but two or three times Frazier had called him Orwell, and I assumed he had guessed. But as we left the orchard, he said, as if it had just occurred to him, "I wonder who he really was."

Since hearing Burris's story, I have done a bit of checking. Orwell died of tuberculosis in a hospital in London in January 1950. There is no doubt about that. His will directed that his body be "buried (not cremated) according to the rites of the Church of England in the nearest convenient cemetery." He was not a religious man, and his request for a church burial was granted only under considerable public pressure. Who it was who turned up in Walden Two later that year pretending to be Eric Arthur Blair, or how well you may feel he played the role of George Orwell, I am not prepared to say. But his exchanges with Frazier, especially those concerning the role of contingencies of reinforcement in daily life, seemed interesting and worthwhile, and that is why I asked Mr. Burris to bring them to you.

chapter 4

Selection
by Consequences

The history of human behavior, if we may take it to begin
with the origin of life on Earth, is possibly exceeded in scope
only by the history of the universe. Like astronomer and cos-
mologist, the historian proceeds only by reconstructing what
may have happened rather than by reviewing recorded facts.
The story presumably began not with a big bang, but with
that extraordinary moment when a molecule that had the
power to reproduce itself came into existence. It was then that
selection by consequences made its appearance as a causal
mode. Reproduction was itself a first consequence, and it led,
through natural selection, to the evolution of cells, organs,
and organisms that reproduced themselves under increasingly diverse conditions.

What we call behavior evolved as a set of functions fur-
thering the interchange between organism and environment.
In a fairly stable world it could be as much a part of the
genetic endowment of a species as digestion, respiration, or
any other biological function. The involvement with the
environment, however, imposed limitations. The behavior

functioned well only under conditions fairly similar to those under which it was selected. Reproduction under a much wider range of conditions became possible with the evolution of two processes through which individual organisms acquired behavior appropriate to novel environments. Through respondent (Pavlovian) conditioning, responses prepared in advance by natural selection could come under the control of new stimuli. Through operant conditioning, new responses could be strengthened (*reinforced*) by events that immediately followed them.

A SECOND KIND OF SELECTION

Operant conditioning is a second kind of selection by consequences. It must have evolved in parallel with two other products of the same contingencies of natural selection—a susceptibility to reinforcement by certain kinds of consequences and a supply of behavior less specifically committed to eliciting or releasing stimuli. (Most operants are selected from behavior that has little or no relation to such stimuli.)

When the selecting consequences are the same, operant conditioning and natural selection work together redundantly. For example, the behavior of a duckling in following its mother is apparently the product not only of natural selection (ducklings tend to move in the direction of large moving objects) but also of an evolved susceptibility to reinforcement by proximity to such an object, as Peterson has shown.[1] The common consequence is that the duckling stays near its mother. (Imprinting is a different process, close to respondent conditioning.)

Because a species that quickly acquires behavior appropriate to a given environment has less need for an innate repertoire, operant conditioning could not only supplement the natural selection of behavior but also replace it. There were advantages favoring such a change. When members of a species eat a certain food simply because eating it has had

---

[1]Neil Peterson, "Control of behavior by presentation of an imprinted stimulus," *Science*, 132 (1960), 1395–96.

survival value, the food does not need to be, and presumably is not, a reinforcer. Similarly, when sexual behavior is simply a product of natural selection, sexual contact does not need to be, and presumably is not, a reinforcer. But when, through the evolution of special susceptibilities, food and sexual contact become reinforcing, new forms of behavior can be set up. New ways of gathering, processing, and ultimately cultivating foods and new ways of behaving sexually or of behaving in ways that lead only eventually to sexual reinforcement can be shaped and maintained. The behavior so conditioned is not necessarily adaptive: Foods are eaten that are not healthful, and sexual behavior strengthened that is not related to procreation.

Much of the behavior studied by ethologists—courtship, mating, care of the young, intraspecific aggression, defense of territory, and so on—is social. It is within easy range of natural selection because other members of a species are one of the most stable features of the environment of a species. Innate social repertoires are supplemented by imitation. By running when others run, for example, an animal responds to "releasing stimuli" to which it has not itself been exposed. A different kind of imitation, with a much wider range, results from the fact that contingencies of reinforcement that induce one organism to behave in a given way will often affect another organism when it behaves in the same way. An imitative repertoire that brings the imitator under the control of new contingencies is therefore acquired.

The human species presumably became much more social when its vocal musculature came under operant control. Cries of alarm, mating calls, aggressive threats, and other kinds of vocal behavior can be modified through operant conditioning, but apparently only with respect to the occasions upon which they occur and their rate of occurrence.[2]

The ability of the human species to acquire new forms through selection by consequences presumably resulted from the evolution of a special innervation of the vocal mus-

---

[2]The imitative vocal behavior of certain birds may be an exception, but if it has selective consequences comparable to those of cries of alarm or mating calls, they are obscure. The vocal behavior of the parrot is shaped, at best, by a trivial consequence, involving the resemblance between sounds produced and sounds heard.

culature, together with a supply of vocal behavior not strongly under the control of eliciting or "releasing" stimuli, such as the babbling of children, from which verbal operants are selected. No new susceptibility to reinforcement was needed because the consequences of verbal behavior are distinguished only by the fact that they are mediated by other people.[3]

The development of environmental control of the vocal musculature greatly extended the help one person receives from others. By behaving verbally people cooperate more successfully in common ventures. By taking advice, heeding warnings, following instructions, and observing rules, they profit from what others have already learned. Ethical practices are strengthened by being codified in laws, and special techniques of ethical and intellectual self-management are devised and taught. Self-observation or awareness emerges when one person asks another a question such as "What are you going to do?" or "Why did you do that?" The invention of the alphabet spread these advantages over great distances and periods of time. They have long been said to give the human species its unique position, although it is possible that what is unique is simply the extension of operant control to the vocal musculature.

A THIRD KIND OF SELECTION

Verbal behavior greatly increased the importance of a third kind of selection by consequences, the evolution of social environments—cultures. The process presumably begins at the level of the individual. A better way of making a tool, growing food, or teaching a child is reinforced by its consequence—the tool, the food, or a useful helper, respectively. A culture evolves when practices originating in this way contribute to the success of the practicing group in solving its problems. It is the effect on the group, not the reinforcing consequences for individual members, that is responsible for the evolution of the culture.

---

[3]See B. F. Skinner, *Verbal behavior* (New York: Appleton, 1957).

In summary, then, human behavior is the joint product of (1) the contingencies of survival responsible for the natural selection of the species and (2) the contingencies of reinforcement responsible for the repertoires acquired by its members, including (3) the special contingencies maintained by an evolved social environment. (Ultimately, of course, it is all a matter of natural selection, since operant conditioning is an evolved process, of which cultural practices are special applications.)

SIMILARITIES AND DIFFERENCES

Each of the three levels of variation and selection has its own discipline—the first, biology; the second, psychology; and the third, anthropology. Only the second, operant conditioning, occurs at a speed at which it can be observed from moment to moment. Biologists and anthropologists study the processes through which variations arise and are selected, but they merely reconstruct the evolution of a species or culture. Operant conditioning is selection in progress. It resembles a hundred million years of natural selection or a thousand years of the evolution of a culture compressed into a very short period of time.

The immediacy of operant conditioning has certain practical advantages. For example, when a currently adaptive feature is presumably too complex to have occurred in its present form as a single variation, it is usually explained as the product of a sequence of simpler variations, each having its own survival value. It is standard practice in evolutionary theory to look for such sequences, and anthropologists and historians have reconstructed the stages through which moral and ethical codes, art, music, literature, science, technology, and so on, have presumably evolved. A complex operant, however, can actually be shaped through successive approximation if we arrange a graded series of contingencies of reinforcement.[4]

---

[4]Patterns of innate behavior too complex to have arisen as single variations may have been shaped by geologic changes due to plate tectonics: B. F. Skinner, "The shaping of phylogenic behavior," *Acta Neurobiologiae Experimentalis*, 35 (1975), 409; also published in *Journal of the Experimental Analysis of Behavior*, 24 (1975), 117–20; reprinted

A current question at level 1 has parallels at levels 2 and 3. If natural selection is a valid principle, why do many species remain unchanged for thousands or even millions of years? Presumably, the answer is either that no variations have occurred or that those that occurred were not selected by the prevailing contingencies. Similar questions may be asked at levels 2 and 3. Why do people continue to do things the same way for many years, and why do groups of people continue to observe old practices for centuries? The answers are presumably the same: either new variations (new forms of behavior or new practices) have not appeared or those that have appeared have not been selected by the prevailing contingencies (of reinforcement or of the survival of the group). At all three levels a sudden, possibly extensive, change is explained as being due to new variations selected by prevailing contingencies or to new contingencies. Competition with other species, persons, or cultures may or may not be involved. Structural constraints may also play a part at all three levels.

Another issue is the definition or identity of a species, person, or culture. Traits in a species and practices in a culture are transmitted from generation to generation, but reinforced behavior is "transmitted" only in the sense of remaining part of the repertoire of the individual. Where species and cultures are defined by restrictions imposed upon transmission—by genes and chromosomes and, say, geographical isolation, respectively—a problem of definition (or identity) arises at level 2, but only when different contingencies of reinforcement create different repertoires, persons, or selves.

TRADITIONAL EXPLANATORY SCHEMES

As a causal mode, selection by consequences was discovered very late in the history of science—indeed, less than a century and a half ago—and it is still not fully recognized or under-

---

in B. F. Skinner, *Reflections on behaviorism and society* (Englewood Cliffs, N.J.: Prentice-Hall, 1978).

stood, especially at levels 2 and 3. The facts for which it is responsible have been forced into the causal pattern of classical mechanics, and many of the explanatory schemes elaborated in the process must now be discarded. Some of them have great prestige and are strongly defended at all three levels. Here are four examples:

A prior act of creation.   (1) Natural selection replaces a very special creator and is still challenged because it does so. (2) Operant conditioning provides a similarly controversial account of the ("voluntary") behavior traditionally attributed to a creative mind. (3) The evolution of a social environment replaces the supposed origin of a culture as a social contract or of social practices as commandments.

Purpose or intention.   Only past consequences figure in selection. (1) A particular species does not have eyes in order that its members may see better; it has them because certain members, undergoing variation, were able to see better and hence were more likely to transmit the variation. (2) The consequences of operant behavior are not what the behavior is now for; they are merely similar to the consequences that have shaped and maintained it. (3) People do not observe particular practices in order that the group will be more likely to survive; they observe them because groups that induced their members to do so survived and transmitted them.

Certain essences.   (1) A molecule that could reproduce itself and evolve into cell, organ, and organism, was alive as soon as it came into existence without the help of a vital principle called life. (2) Operant behavior is shaped and brought under the control of the environment without the intervention of a principle of mind. (To suppose that thought appeared as a variation, like a morphological trait in genetic theory, is to invoke an unnecessarily large *saltum*.) (3) Social environments generate self-knowledge ("consciousness") and self-management ("reason") without help from a group mind or Zeitgeist.

To say this is not to reduce life, mind, and Zeitgeist to physics; it is simply to recognize the expendability of essences.

The facts are as they have always been. To say that selection by consequences is a causal mode found only in living things is to say only that selection (or the "replication with error" that made it possible) defines *living*. (A computer can be programmed to model natural selection, operant conditioning, or the evolution of a culture, but only when constructed and programmed by a living thing.) The physical basis of natural selection is now fairly clear; the corresponding basis of operant conditioning, and hence of the evolution of cultures, has yet to be discovered.

Certain definitions of good and value. (1) What is good for the species is whatever promotes the survival of its members until offspring have been born and, possibly, cared for. Traits that have survival value (such as parental care) are called good. (2) Things that reinforce behavior because of innate susceptibilities to reinforcement are said to taste good, feel good, and so on. Behavior is called good if it has that kind of reinforcing consequence. (3) "Good" is a verbal reinforcer, used to transmit cultural practices that promote the survival of the practicing group. These are not, of course, traditional definitions; they do not recognize a world of value distinct from a world of fact, and for other reasons to be noted shortly, they are challenged.

ALTERNATIVES TO SELECTION

Attempts are often made to convert selection into the causal mode of classical mechanics. "Selection pressure" is an example. It suggests forcing a change. A more serious example is the metaphor of storage. Contingencies of selection necessarily lie in the past; they are not acting when their effect is observed. To provide a current cause, it has therefore been assumed they are stored (usually as "information") and later retrieved. Thus, (1) genes and chromosomes are said to contain the information needed by the fertilized egg in order to grow into a mature organism. But a cell does not consult a store of information in order to learn how to change; it changes because of features that are the product of a history of variation and selection, a product that is not well represented by the metaphor of storage. (2) People are said to store information about contingencies of reinforcement and retrieve it for use on later occasions. But they do not consult copies of earlier contingencies to discover how to behave; they behave in given ways because they have been changed by those contingencies. The contingencies can perhaps be inferred from the changes they have worked, but they no longer exist. (3) A possibly legitimate use of storage in the evolution of cultures may be responsible for these mistakes. Parts of the social environment maintained and transmitted by a group are quite literally stored in documents, artifacts, and other products of that behavior.

Other causal forces serving in lieu of selection have been sought in the structure of a species, person, or culture. Organization is an example. (1) Until recently, most biologists argued that organization distinguished living from nonliving things. (2) According to Gestalt psychologists and others, both perceptions and acts occur in certain inevitable ways because of their organization. (3) Many anthropologists and linguists appeal to the organization of cultural and linguistic practices. It is true that all species, persons, and cultures are highly organized, but no principle of organization explains their being so. Both the organization and the effects attributed to it can be traced to the respective contingencies of selection. The same may be said of structure.

Another example is growth. Developmentalism is structuralism to which time or age has been added as an independent variable. (1) There was evidence before Darwin that species had "developed." (2) Cognitive psychologists have argued that concepts develop in the child in certain fixed orders, and Freud said the same for the psychosexual functions. (3) Some anthropologists have contended that cultures must evolve through a prescribed series of stages, and Marx said as much in his insistence upon historical determinism. But at all three levels the changes can be explained by the "development" of contingencies of selection. New contingencies of natural selection come within range as a species evolves; new contingencies of reinforcement begin to operate as behavior becomes more complex; and new contingencies of survival are dealt with by increasingly effective cultures.

SELECTION NEGLECTED

The causal force attributed to structure as a surrogate of selection causes trouble when a feature at one level is said to explain a similar feature at another; the historical priority of natural selection usually gives it a special place. Sociobiology offers many examples. Behavior described as the defense of territory may be due to (1) contingencies of survival in the evolution of a species, possibly involving food supplies or breeding practices; (2) contingencies of reinforcement for the individual, possibly involving a share of the reinforcers available in the territory; or (3) contingencies maintained by the cultural practices of a group, promoting behavior that contributes to the survival of the group. Similarly, altruistic behavior (1) may evolve through, say, kin selection; (2) may be shaped and maintained by contingencies of reinforcement arranged by those for whom the behavior works an advantage; or (3) may be generated by cultures that for example, induce individuals to suffer or die as heroes or martyrs. The contingencies of selection at the three levels are quite different, and the structural similarity does not attest to a common generative principle.

When a causal force is assigned to structure, selection tends to be neglected. Many issues that arise in morals and ethics can be resolved if we specify the level of selection. What is good for the individual or culture may have bad consequences for the species, as when sexual reinforcement leads to overpopulation or the reinforcing amenities of civilization to the exhaustion of resources; what is good for the species or culture may be bad for the individual, as when practices designed to control procreation or preserve resources restrict individual freedom; and so on. There is nothing inconsistent or contradictory about these uses of "good" or "bad," or about other value judgments, as long as the level of selection is specified.

AN INITIATING AGENT

The role of selection by consequences has been particularly resisted because there is no place for the initiating agent suggested by classical mechanics. We try to identify such an agent when we say (1) that a species adapts to an environment (rather than that the environment selects the adaptive traits); (2) that an individual adjusts to a situation (rather than that the situation shapes and maintains adjusted behavior); and (3) that a group of people solve a problem raised by certain circumstances (rather than that the circumstances select the cultural practice that yields a solution).

The question of an initiating agent is raised in its most acute form by our own place in this history. Darwin and Spencer thought that selection would necessarily lead to perfection, but species, persons, and cultures all perish when they cannot cope with rapid change, and our species now appears to be threatened. Must we wait for selection to solve the problems of overpopulation, exhaustion of resources, pollution of the environment, and a possible nuclear holocaust, or can we take explicit steps to make our future more secure? In the latter case, must we not in some sense transcend selection?

We could be said to intervene in the process of selection when as geneticists we change the characteristics of a species or create new species, or when as governors, employers, or teachers we change the behavior of persons, or when as behavioral scientists we design new cultural practices. But in none of these ways do we escape selection by consequences. In the first place, we can work only through variation and selection. At level 1 we can change genes and chromosomes or contingencies of survival, as in selective breeding. At level 2 we can introduce new forms of behavior—for example, by showing or telling people what to do with respect to relevant contingencies—or construct and maintain new selective contingencies. At level 3 we can introduce new cultural practices or, rarely, arrange special contingencies of survival—for example, to preserve a traditional practice. But having done these things, we must wait for selection to occur. (There is a special reason why these limitations are significant. It is often said that the human species is now able to control its own genetics, its own behavior, and its own destiny. But it does not do so in the sense in which the term *control* is used in classical mechanics, and for the very reason that living things are not machines: Selection by consequences makes the difference.) In the second place, we must consider the possibility that our behavior in intervening is itself a product of selection. We tend to regard ourselves as initiating agents only because we know or remember so little about our genetic and environmental histories.

Although we can now predict many of the contingencies of selection to which the human species will probably be exposed at all three levels and can specify behavior that will satisfy many of them, we have failed to establish cultural practices under which much of that behavior is selected and maintained. It is possible that our effort to preserve the role of the individual as an originator is at fault, and that a wider recognition of the role of selection by consequences will make an important difference.

The present scene is not encouraging. Psychology is the discipline of choice at level 2, but few psychologists pay much attention to selection. The existentialists among them are explicitly concerned with the here and now rather than the past and future. Structuralists and developmentalists tend to neglect selective contingencies in their search for causal principles in organization or growth. The conviction that contingencies are stored as information is only one of the reasons why the appeal to cognitive functions is not helpful. The three personae of psychoanalytic theory are in many respects close to our three levels of selection. But the id does not adequately represent the enormous contribution of the natural history of the species; the superego, even with the help of the ego ideal, does not adequately represent the contribution of the social environment to language, self-knowledge, and intellectual and ethical self management; and the ego is a poor likeness of the personal repertoire acquired under the practical contingencies of daily life. The field known as the experimental analysis of behavior has extensively explored selection by consequences, but its conception of human behavior is resisted, and many of its practical applications rejected, precisely because it has no place for a person as an initiating agent. The behavioral sciences at level 3 show similar shortcomings. Anthropology is heavily structural, and political scientists and economists usually treat the individual as a free initiating agent. Philosophy and letters offer no promising leads.

The proper recognition of the selective action of the environment will require a change in our conception of the origin of behavior, a change perhaps as extensive as that of our former conceptions of the origin of species. As long as we cling to the view that a person is an initiating doer, actor, or causer of behavior, we shall probably continue to neglect the conditions that must be changed if we are to solve our problems.[5]

---

[5] See my *Beyond freedom and dignity* (New York: Knopf, 1971).

chapter 5

The Evolution of Behavior

ಶ್ರಾಣ್ಯಾ ಶ್ರಾಣ್ಯಾ ಶ್ರಾಣ್ಯಾ ಶ್ರಾಣ್ಯಾ

Evolutionary theorists not only point to the survival value of the present structure and function of an organism; they try to reconstruct earlier stages, which should also have had survival value. An example of current interest is the flight of birds. Feathers may have evolved first as thermal insulation, but what about wings? Were they adaptations of forelimbs that first helped ground animals run faster or tree animals leap from branch to branch or from branch to ground? (Even when a feature first evolved because of consequences quite different from those that explain its current survival value, a plausible early history is still needed.) Among the features to be explained in this way is behavior. The current survival value of reflexes and the released patterns of behavior studied by ethologists may be clear, but can we construct plausible sequences through which these patterns of behavior could have evolved, maintaining survival value at every stage?

The first behavior was presumably simple movement—like that of the amoeba reaching out into new territory and hence increasing its chances of finding materials necessary for its survival. Then, presumably, came sensing, which would enable the organism to move away from harmful stimuli and closer to useful materials. The assignment of different organs to sensing and moving should have led to the evolution of connecting structures, and eventually to tropisms and reflexes.

The released behavior patterns studied by ethologists also presumably evolved through increasingly complex stages. It is unlikely that many current instances occurred first in their present state as variations which were then selected by survival. In my paper "The Shaping of Phylogenic Behavior" I suggested that well-known geological changes could have supplied some of the necessary sequences of contingencies.[1] It would not be hard to teach a fish to jump from a lower level to a higher one. One could reinforce swimming across an underwater barrier, slowly raise the barrier until it reached the surface, and then raise it so that it became the wall of a second tank. As the levels of water slowly separated, the fish would jump with greater and greater force. Something of the same sort, over a very different time span, may have happened if the shallow, graveled bottom of a river in which salmon breed moved upstream as the river changed and as rapids and falls intervened between the graveled bottom and the ocean.

A different geological change has been suggested to explain the behavior of the turtles that feed along the coast of Brazil but swim more than a thousand miles to Ascension Island, where they breed.[2] Apparently they once swam to nearer islands, which have disappeared. A third example is the behavior of the Atlantic eel, which travels from either American or European rivers to a breeding ground near the Sargasso Sea. These long journeys are taken only once, and it is quite unlikely that they could have occurred first in their present form as variations. When North America and Europe first separated, however, the distances must have been short.

---

[1] B. F. Skinner, "The shaping of phylogenic behavior," *Acta Neurobiologiae Experimentalis,* 35 (1975), 409–15.

[2] A. Carr, "Adaptive aspects of the scheduled travel of *Chelonia,*" in *Animal orientation and navigation,* ed. R. M. Storm (Corvallis: Oregon State University Press, 1967), pp. 35–55.

The present behavior could have evolved as each generation went at most a few centimeters farther than the preceding one.

Like most evolutionary theories, these are speculations, but they appeal to known geological changes that could provide the conditions under which complex behavior would be shaped. So far as I know, ethologists have not given very much attention to plausible histories of this sort. Some, indeed, have questioned whether reproduction with variation can explain complex behavior without appeal to mental processes. There is a heron, for example, that fishes by touching the surface of the water with a feather and seizing the fish that rises to this simulation of an insect. Does the heron not show some of the thought processes of the human angler? But the journey of the eel from the Nile River to the Sargasso Sea, a quarter of the way around the earth, is a much more complex example of innate behavior and is much harder to explain in "cognitive" terms. Anyone who has seen a slip of a plant grow into a complete plant with flowers and fruit, an achievement also hard to attribute to mental life, will have no difficulty in accepting the role of natural selection in the origin of behavior, no matter how complex.

Social behavior raises a special problem when two interrelated but different kinds of behavior appear to evolve together. If bees returning to the hive dance in ways used by other bees in finding sources of food, what could have been the survival value of the dance before other bees responded to it, and how could a response have evolved before returning bees danced? We must assume that returning bees behaved in ways related to the location of food for reasons unrelated to the food. A bee that had come a long way might show fatigue, a bee coming in a particular direction might make circular phototropic movements, and so on. Once the responses of other bees to these stimuli had evolved, further refinements could occur.[3]

---

[3] A similar explanation is needed for the evolution of pheromones. Why were scent trails laid down before other members of the species responded to them, and how could responding to them have evolved if there were no trails? We must assume either that a trail was laid for other reasons (like the trail followed by a bloodhound), in which case responding to it as a pheromone evolved first, or that some trace left by an animal was

BEHAVIORAL PROCESSES:
IMITATION AND MODELING

The evolution of the processes through which behavior changes also needs to be explained. An early example must have been imitation. A structural definition (behaving as another organism is behaving) will not suffice: The dog chasing the rabbit is not imitating the rabbit. Phylogenic imitation could be defined as behaving as another organism is behaving for no alternative environmental reason. But some other reason may first have been necessary. Consider a group of grazing animals subject to frequent predation. Each exhibits a strong tendency to run, in response not only to predation but to stimuli correlated with predators. An example of the latter could be the sudden running of one or more other members of the group, already responding to the predator. At that stage the behavior would not be imitation; it would be released by either of two stimuli—the sight of a predator or the sight of another animal suddenly running. But a variation as a result of which one organism imitated another would then have had survival value as redundant support. As the process developed, the imitative model could take full control, and the imitator would then simply do what another animal was doing and for no other reason.

Once imitation has evolved, contingencies of selection exist in which modeling could evolve. A young bird will eventually fly by itself, but if it flies sooner when parent birds fly, and if early flying has survival value, then parental modeling should evolve, the parent birds flying often and in particularly conspicuous ways that are easily imitated.

RESPONDENT CONDITIONING

As evolved processes through which behavior changes during the lifetime of the individual, imitation and modeling prepare

---

followed for other reasons (because it smelled like food, for example), in which case leaving a trace as a pheromone evolved first. Once the leaving of traces evolved because of what happened when other members of the species responded to them, or once traces left for no particular reason were followed because of what then happened, the character of the pheromone could change.

the individual only for behavior that has already been acquired by the organisms that model it. Other processes have evolved that bring the individual under the control of environments to which the individual alone is exposed. One is respondent (Pavlovian or classical) conditioning. Under what conditions could it have evolved?

Let us consider Pavlov's classical example: A bell frequently followed by the delivery of food eventually begins to elicit salivation. The unconditioned salivation is an evolved reflex. The commonest stimuli are substances in the mouth, but in a stable environment salivation at the mere appearnace of a particular food should also have evolved, as seizing and eating the food evolved in response to the same stimuli. The contingencies would favor a stronger response to taste, however. Respondent conditioning could have begun as a variation that made the visible features of food *slightly more likely* to elicit salivation. Saliva would then have been secreted in response to the sight of food, both as a weak reflex arising from natural selection and as a conditioned reflex. The conditioned version could take over in response to a stimulus (e.g., a bell) that had no effect due to natural selection.

Salivation does not suggest strong survival value, and the argument is more convincing for sweating and the acceleration in pulse rate associated with vigorous action. An evolved tendency to fight or run away at the sight of a predator could be accompanied by an evolved tendency to sweat and increase the pulse rate, but there would be more sweating and a more rapid pulse during the actual flight or attack. If early sweating and an increased pulse rate helped prepare for effective flight or attack, variations leading to the process of respondent conditioning would have had survival value.

In these examples, respondent conditioning is explained as a supplementary increase in the strength of reflexes that have not fully evolved. The explanation is supported by certain features of respondent conditioning that are often overlooked. The Pavlovian conditioned reflex has no survival value unless it is followed by the unconditioned reflex. Although one can demonstrate that salivation is eventually elicited by a bell, there is no advantage to the organism unless food follows. Similarly, an inclination to sweat or increase heart rate in response to the appearance of a predator also has no value unless vigorous action follows.

The scope of respondent conditioning is much broader than its role in the conditioned reflex. Releasers, studied by ethologists, are conditioned in more or less the same way, and imprinting is at least similar. There is obvious survival value in the behavior of a young duckling as it follows its mother. The features of the releasing object could have been sharply defined, but a lesser demand is placed on the genes if following is released by any large moving object. In the world of the duckling that object is almost always the mother. The looser specification suffices because the mother duck is a consistent feature of the duckling's natural environment. The imprinting is a kind of statistical confirmation of a less-than-specific genetic instruction.

OPERANT CONDITIONING

A different explanation is needed for operant conditioning. Under what conditions could the smallest possible variation contribute to the evolution of the process? Innate behavior has consequences ultimately related to survival. The hand is withdrawn from a painful stimulus presumably because the stimulus is potentially damaging; the response promotes survival by preventing damage. Any slight change resulting in the quicker termination of subsequent damage should have survival value, and operant conditioning through negative reinforcement would be such a change. The operant response would be an exact duplicate of the phylogenic response, and the strengthening consequences would be the same, contributing to the survival of the individual and hence of the species through both natural selection and an evolved susceptibility to reinforcement by a reduction in painful stimuli.

A similar argument can be made for positive reinforcement. If eating a particular kind of food has had survival value (such as that explaining the behavior of eating the food), an increased tendency to eat because the taste of the food has become a reinforcer should also have had survival value. Both the topography of the behavior and the immediate consequence (ingestion of a particular food) would be the same, but there would be two consequences: one related to natural selection and one to an evolved susceptibility to operant reinforcement by a particular taste. Once the process of operant conditioning had evolved, topographies of behavior having less and less resemblance to phylogenic behavior could have been affected, and eventually behavior could have emerged in novel environments that were not stable enough to support it through natural selection.

Two other stages in the evolution of operant behavior need to be considered. Once the process existed, a susceptibility to reinforcement by new forms of stimulation could have evolved. It would have been supplemented by a new role for respondent conditioning—the conditioning of reinforcers. Stimuli that frequently precede unconditioned reinforcers could begin to have reinforcing effects in both respondent and operant conditioning.

A second stage may have been the evolution of unconditioned behavior that had no survival value of its own but was available for selection through operant reinforcement. Such behavior would enable the individual to develop a much wider repertoire of behavior appropriate to novel environments. The human infant shows a large repertoire of such uncommitted behavior.

Many current contingencies of reinforcement resemble contingencies of survival. We behave in a given way both because we are members of a given species and because we live in a world in which certain contingencies of reinforcement prevail. Thus, we avoid going over a cliff, we dodge objects, we imitate others, we struggle against restraint, we turn toward a movement seen out of the corner of an eye—and all for two kinds of reasons: contingencies of survival and contingencies of reinforcement. It would be hard to say how much of the strength of the behavior is due to each. Only a first instance can be said to be necessarily innate, and first instances are hard to spot. An example of current interest is aggression. We may have an innate repertoire of aggressive behavior, but similar behavior is generated by many contingencies of reinforcement. It does not matter whether a given instance is phylogenic or ontogenic unless we are concerned with doing something about it. If we are, we must identify the variables to be changed.

In the human species, operant conditioning has very largely replaced natural selection. A long infancy gives the ontogenic process greater scope, and its role in adapting to very unstable environments is a great advantage. Nevertheless, the process is not untouched by environmental changes. As I have pointed out elsewhere,[4] the human susceptibilities to reinforcement by sugar and salt, sexual contact, and signs of aggressive damage may once have had much greater survival values than they have now. Technological advances in the production, storage, and distribution of foodstuffs, in the control of pestilence, and in the improvement of weapons may have made these susceptibilities more likely to be lethal.

Just as very complex innate behavior has led to an appeal to cognitive processes, so it is often argued that operant conditioning cannot account for complex learned behavior. Animals as well as people are said to transcend the shaping and maintenance of behavior by contingencies of reinforcement and to show insight, the development of concepts, and other cognitive processes. Such claims are vulnerable to demonstrations that operant conditioning will suffice. For example, Epstein, Lanza, Starr, and I have simulated a variety of complex cognitive processes in pigeons.[5] Not only can such behavior be attributed to fortuitous contingencies of reinforcement, it can be produced by arranging the necessary contingencies.

It has also been said (by Thorndike, for example) that things reinforce because of the way they feel, but certainly the reinforcing effect must have evolved first. Only when that had happened would things have been felt as, and called, pleasing and satisfying. Perhaps we should speak of feelings only when

---

[4]B. F. Skinner, "Contingencies of reinforcement in the design of a culture," *Behavioral Science*, 11 (1966), 159–66.

[5]R. Epstein, R. P. Lanza, and B. F. Skinner, "Symbolic communications between two pigeons (*Columbia livia domestica*)," *Science*, 207 (1980), 543–45; R. Epstein, R. P. Lanza, and B. F. Skinner, "Self-awareness in the pigeon," *Science*, 212 (1981), 695–96; R. Epstein and B. F. Skinner, "The spontaneous use of memoranda by pigeons," *Behavior*

what is felt is reinforcing. If we pull our hand away from a hot plate simply as a reflex, the reduction in painful stimulation plays no current role. Perhaps it is only because the behavior is reinforced by the same reduction that we say that the stimulation hurts. The same may be true of positive reinforcers. Insects copulating simply as phylogenic behavior might not be "enjoying themselves."

The conditions under which operant conditioning evolved are helpful in understanding its nature. Selection did not need to respect how a bit of behavior produced a consequence; any immediate consequence would have sufficed. Immediacy was essential for other reasons. Deferred reinforcers have a more powerful effect upon intervening behavior, and behavior must be in progress if it is to be changed by a consequence. The claim that behavior is affected by a general melioration, optimization, or maximization of a reinforcing condition conflicts with these principles, and the evidence should be reexamined—so that we can be sure, for example, that gaps between behavior and deferred consequences are not bridged by conditioned reinforcers.

A concept of optimization is like the concept of health. The healing of a wound restores a normal condition of the body, and the normal condition favors survival. But healing does not occur because it promotes survival; it occurs because certain structures in the individual have evolved because they have promoted survival. Similarly, in a hungry organism an operant is reinforced by the receipt of food. The food reduces a state of hunger and contributes to the survival of the individual and species. But the operant does not occur because it reduces hunger; it occurs because certain behavioral processes have evolved when a reduction in hunger has contributed to the survival of the species. Behavior is not reinforced by the melioration, optimization, or maximization of anything. It is reinforced through evolved processes which have the ultimate effects to which those terms refer.

Analysis Letters, 1 (1981), 241–46; R. P. Lanza, J. Starr, and B. F. Skinner, " 'Lying' in the pigeon," *Journal of the Experimental Analysis of Behavior*, 38 (1982), 201–3.

THE EVOLUTION OF CULTURAL PRACTICES

Operant imitation requires no new evolved process. When organisms are behaving because of prevailing contingencies of reinforcement, similar behavior in another organism is likely to be reinforced by the same contingencies. A general conditioned tendency to behave as others behave supplements phylogenic imitation. Operant modeling then follows: When the behavior of another person is important, modeling is reinforced when the other person imitates.

Imitation and modeling play important roles in transmitting the results of exceptional contingencies of reinforcement. Some of the great human achievements were due to extraordinarily lucky accidents. Other people came under the control of the same fortuitous contingencies through imitation, and the behavior was transmitted even more rapidly by modeling. The human species made further progress in the transmission of what had already been learned when its vocal apparatus came under operant control.

A culture may be defined as the contingencies of social reinforcement maintained by a group. As such it evolves in its own way, as new cultural practices, however they arise, contribute to the survival of the group and are perpetuated because they do so. The evolution of cultures is of no further relevance here because no new behavioral processes are involved.

chapter 6

The Evolution
of Verbal Behavior

ॐॐॐॐॐ

Evolutionary theory has always been plagued by scantiness of evidence. We see the products of evolution but not much of the process. Most of the story happened long ago, and little remains of the early stages. Especially few traces of behavior remain; only recently were there artifacts that could endure. Verbal behavior left no artifacts until the appearance of writing, and that was at a very late stage. We shall probably never know precisely what happened, but we ought to be able to say what might have happened—that is, what kinds of variations and what kinds of contingencies of selection could have brought verbal behavior into existence. Speculation about natural selection is supported by current research on genetics; the evolution of a social environment, or culture, is supported by the experimental analysis of behavior.

Strictly speaking, verbal behavior does not evolve. It is the product of a verbal environment, or what linguists call a language, and it is the verbal environment that evolves. Because a verbal environment is composed of listeners, it is understandable that linguists emphasize the listener. (A question often asked, for example, is "How is it possible for a person to understand a potentially infinite number of sentences?" In contrast, a behavior analyst asks, "How is it possible for a person to *say* a potentially infinite number of sentences?") This paper, then, is about the evolution of a verbal environment as the source of the behavior of a speaker.

The plausibility of a reconstruction depends in part upon the size of the variations that are assumed to have occurred: The smaller the variations, the more plausible the explanation. Web making by the spider, for example, could scarcely have appeared all at once in its present form as a variation. That it evolved in a series of small steps is more plausible. The excretion that eventually became silk may have begun as a coating for eggs. It worked better when it took the form of fibers with which eggs could be wrapped rather than coated. The fibers helped the spiders keep from falling as they worked, and as the fibers grew stronger, they might have enabled the spiders to lift and lower themselves. Strands left behind might have caught insects, which the spiders ate. The more strands that were left, the more insects the spiders caught. Some patterns of strands caught more than others. And so on. That may not be exactly what happened, but it is easier to believe than the appearance of web making as a sudden, single variation.

The evolution of behavior is also more plausible if regarded as the product of a series of small variations and selections. The process is rather like the shaping of operant behavior through small changes in contingencies of reinforcement, and what we have learned about the operant process has helped us understand the genetic process in spite of the great differences between them.

PHYLOGENIC "SIGNALING"

The word *sign* does not commit its user to any theory of language. Smoke is a sign of fire and dark clouds a sign of rain. The growl of a vicious dog is a sign of danger. Organisms come to respond to signs through well-known behavioral processes. To *signal* is to make a sign; we account for signaling by noting the consequences that would have followed. Fire and rain do not signal, but dogs do if what other animals have done when dogs have growled has played a part in the selection of growling. There are difficulties in explaining the evolution of even that relatively simple example, however, and other kinds of "signaling" raise other problems.

Organisms must have profited from each other's behavior at a very early stage through imitation. To imitate is more than to do what another organism is doing. Pigeons foraging in a park are not imitating each other to any great extent; they are acting independently under similar environmental contingencies. To imitate is to act as another organism is acting because similar consequences have then followed. The evolution of the process can be traced to plausible selective consequences: The contingencies responsible for the behavior imitated may affect another organism when it behaves in the same way. Thus, if one of two grazing animals sees a predator and runs, the other is more likely to escape if it runs too, although it has not seen the predator. Running whenever another organism runs usually has survival value.

It was only after a tendency to imitate had evolved that contingencies existed for the evolution of the reciprocal process of modeling. A young bird that would eventually learn to fly without help learns sooner when it imitates a flying bird, Its parents can speed the process by flying where the young bird can see them and in ways that are easily imitated. To say that the parents are "showing their young how to fly" adds nothing to such an account and may imply more than is actually involved.

The evolution of other kinds of reciprocally helpful behavior is not as easily explained. For example, what would have been the survival value of the dance of the honeybee that was returning from good forage before other bees responded to the dance, and how could responding to it have evolved before bees danced? (The question is not raised by imitation and modeling, because the contingencies that account for imitation do not require modeling.) We must assume that the distance or the direction in which the returning bees traveled had some other effect on their behavior. Perhaps signs of fatigue varied with the distance or phototropic movements varied according to the position of the sun on their return. Once reciprocal behavior had evolved, further variations could make it more effective. Returning bees could dance in more conspicuous ways and other bees could respond more accurately to features of the dance. It is often said that bees have a language, that they "tell each other where good forage is to be found," that the dance "conveys information," and so on. Such expressions, useful enough in casual discourse, add nothing to an explanation in terms of natural selection and may obscure the processes at issue.

ONTOGENIC "SIGNALING"

Contingencies of reinforcement resemble contingencies of survival in many ways. Animals learn to imitate when by doing what others are doing they are affected by the same contingencies—of reinforcement rather than of survival. Once that has happened, contingencies exist in which others learn to model—to behave in ways that can be more easily imitated. If, for example, a door can be opened only by being slid to one side, rather than pushed or pulled, a person will slide it after seeing another person do so, although the other person is not necessarily modeling the behavior. In such an example, both parties may exhibit traces of phylogenic imitation or modeling, but operant contingencies would suffice. A modeler not close to the door could make the kind of movement that would open it if he *were* close—as a gesture. Again, to say that the modeler is "showing the other how to open the door" is useful in casual discourse but potentially troublesome in a scientific account.

When a gesture is not a kind of modeling, we must ask what could have reinforced it before anyone responded appropriately, and how anyone could have learned to respond before it had come into existence as a gesture. How, for example, could the gesture with which a traffic officer stops an approaching car have been acquired before people stopped in response to it, and how could people have learned to stop before anyone gestured that way? As in the case of the bees, other contingencies related to stopping are needed, and of course they are not hard to find. One person can stop another by placing a hand on his chest; a person who finds such contact aversive will stop on later occasions before contact is made. The movement of arm and hand changes from a practical response to a gesture. Once that has happened, the topography can change until it would have little or no physical effect.

The gesture that means "Come here" is another example. It presumably originated as practical pulling but became effective as a gesture when people who were pulled moved quickly to avoid physical contact. The topography of the gesture still varies with distance, possibly because of its visibility, but also as if some practical work remained to be done: When the parties are far apart, the whole arm is moved; when they are fairly near, only the forearm; and when they are close, only the hand or just a finger.

VOCAL BEHAVIOR

The human species took a crucial step forward when its vocal musculature came under operant control in the production of speech sounds. Indeed, it is possible that all the distinctive achievements of the species can be traced to that one genetic change. Other species behave vocally, of course, and the behavior is sometimes modified slightly during the lifetime of the individual (as in birdsong, for example), but there the principal contingencies of selection have remained phylogenic—either physical (as in echo location) or social. Parrots and a few other birds imitate human speech, but it is hard to change this behavior or bring it under stimulus control through operant conditioning.

Some of the organs involved in the production of speech sounds were already subject to operant conditioning. The diaphragm must have participated in controlled breathing, the tongue and jaw in chewing and swallowing, the jaw and teeth in biting and tearing, and the lips in sipping and sucking, all of which could be changed through operant conditioning. Only the vocal cords and pharynx seem to have served no prior operant function. They presumably evolved as organs for the production of phylogenic calls and cries. The crucial step in the evolution of verbal behavior appears, then, to have been the genetic change that brought them under the control of operant conditioning and made possible the coordination of all these systems in the production of speech sounds. Since other primates have not taken that step, the change in man was presumably recent. The possibility that it may not yet be complete in all members of the species may explain why there are so many speech disorders, and perhaps even so many individual differences in complex verbal behavior, such as mathematics.

Vocal behavior must have had several advantages in natural selection. Sounds are effective in the dark, around corners, and when listeners are not looking, and they can be made when the hands are busy with other things. There are special advantages, however, in large operant repertoires, especially the enormous variety of available speech sounds. Gestures are not as conspicuously different as speech sounds and hence are fewer in number, and the sounds one produces are more like the sounds one hears than the gestures one makes are like the gestures one sees (because they are seen from a different point of view). One learns to gesture through movement duplication but to speak through product duplication, which is more precise.

It is easier to account for the evolution of operant conditioning if we assume that the first contingencies of reinforcement closely resembled contingencies of natural selection, since only small variations would have been effective if the settings, topographies, and consequences were similar.[1] That could have been true of vocal operants. The cry of a hungry baby, for example, presumably evolved as phylogenic behavior because it alerted the baby's parents. But when through an evolutionary change the attention of the parents began to act as a reinforcer, crying became an operant, and in doing so took on added advantages for the baby and the species. Once existing as an operant, however, crying could appear in circumstances too unstable to figure in natural selection. A baby that was not hungry, for example, could cry

---

[1]See Chapter 5.

in a manner from which the parents would escape by doing things that had no necessary advantage for the species.

A similarity of phylogenic or ontogenic contingencies is not, of course, needed. Coughing, for example, presumably evolved as a reflex that cleared the throat of irritants. But as soon as the vocal musculature came under operant control, coughing could be affected by a different consequence, such as the attention of a listener. If listeners continued to respond, the topography could change until it had no effect on the throat. The cough would become the verbal operant "Ahem!" That could have happened before the vocal cords came under operant cotrol, and something like it may have been the first move from gesture to vocal, but not voiced, behavior.

Although early vocal operants could have been "primed" in this way by phylogenic behavior, the evolution of operant conditioning appears to have been accompanied by the evolution of a pool of behavior that played no other part in natural selection and was therefore more readily subject to operant reinforcement.[2] An obvious vocal example is the babbling of small children—essentially random sounds that became operants when selected by reinforcers. Verbal behavior drawn from a pool of uncommitted behavior has no connection with phylogenic calls or cries, and in general we have no reason to call it an extension of vocal phylogenic "signaling."

A VOCAL EPISODE

Let us say that two men , A and B, are fishing together. They lower a shallow net containing bait into the water; when a fish swims into the net, it is quickly pulled up. Let us say that A lowers and raises the net and B takes a position from which he can see it more clearly. Anything B does when a fish enters the net will serve as a discriminative stimulus for A, in the presence of which pulling will more often be reinforced by the appearance of a fish in the net. B can model pulling, if he has already learned to model, but nothing more is needed than

---

[2] See Chapter 5.

what we might call a sign of "excitement" at the presence of a fish in the net or a sign of "annoyance" at A's failure to pull. Whatever the behavior, it begins to function as a gesture as soon as it has been reinforced by A's response (and, presumably, by a share of the fish). The behavior patterns of both parties then slowly change as their roles become more sharply defined. B becomes more clearly the observer, moving into the best position to see the fish and gesturing as quickly and as effectively as possible, and A becomes more clearly the actor, watching B more closely and pulling as quickly as possible when B responds.

Let us say that as A and B continue to fish cooperatively, a vocal response (perhaps the undifferentiated "uh," requiring no operant control of the vocal cords) is selected by its convenience for B and by the speed and consistency with which it reaches A. We could then describe the episode in either of two ways. In traditional terms, we could say that "when B says 'Uh,' he is telling A that there is a fish in the net," and that he uses "Uh" as a word that "means 'fish' or refers to a fish." Or we could say that B is "telling A to pull the net," in which case "Uh" means "pull."

Cooperative fishing suggests that A and B share the fish, but the roles of A and B are clearer if one gets the fish and induces the other to behave by other means. If B gets the fish and arranges reinforcing consequences for A, "Uh" would be classified in several different ways according to the kind of consequence arranged. If A pulls because in the past B has punished him for not pulling, "Uh" is a *command*. If B has paid A, it is an *order*. If the two are friends, disposed to help each other, it is a *request*. On the other hand, if A gets the fish and somehow reinforces B's response, "Uh" would be called a "report" or an "announcement" of the presence of a fish in the net. But although these traditional expressions may be useful in casual discourse, they do not take us very far toward a scientific account. The episode is nothing more than an instance of the reciprocal behavior of two individuals, and the contingencies that account for it are clear.

TACTS AND MANDS

We have not yet reached the point at which we can call the response either a *mand* or a *tact*. As those terms are defined in *Verbal Behavior*, the consequences must be generalized. The necessary generalization presumably came about when there were many cooperative activities in which a single object (such as a fish) or a single action (such as pulling) played a part. Fish are picked up, carried, put down, cleaned, cooked, eaten, and so on. Although things sometimes have, as we say, "different names according to what is done with them," a single form should emerge through stimulus generalization. A tact emerges, as the probability of saying "fish" in the presence of a fish, when different instances are followed by different reinforcing consequences, quite apart from any other feature of a particular setting. Perhaps there is then no particular harm in using traditional words and saying that *fish* "refers to a fish" or "means 'fish,'" where the meaning or referent is simply the fish as the principal controlling variable. To say that the speaker *uses the word* to mean "fish" or to refer to a fish is, however, to get ahead of our story.

The nature of a tact as a mere probability of responding is clearer if we do not speak of meaning or reference. Let us say that I am calling on someone whose office wall has a large sailfish mounted on it. I start looking for something in my briefcase. When asked what I am doing, I say "I am fishing for a letter I want to show you." The fish on the wall has strengthened *fish* as a tact and has entered into the choice of a synonym. (If instead there had been a display of guns on the wall, I might have been more likely to say, "I am hunting for a letter.") In such a case we do not say that *fishing* refers to the fish on the wall, even though it has been strengthened by it.

As a mere probability of responding, a tact has the same status as three types of verbal operant that are also not said to mean or refer to their controlling variables. One is echoic (we should have been more likely to say "fishing" if someone had just said "fish"). Another is textual (we should have been more likely to say "fishing" if there had been a sign on the wall reading FISH; and a third is intraverbal (we should have been more likely to say "fishing" if we had just read or heard a word that has frequently occurred in proximity with *fish*). We do not say that *fish* means or refers to fish when it is an echoic, textual, or intraverbal response. If we tend to say so when it is a tact, it is not because there is a different kind of controlling relation between stimulus and response, but rather because the listener responds in more useful ways to the controlling stimulus.

As the mere probability of responding under the control of a stimulus, a tact evolves as a product of many instances in which a response of a given form has been reinforced in the presence of a given stimulus in many different states of deprivation or aversive stimulation. When tacts are taught as "the names of things," teachers use a generalized reinforcer— such as "Good!" or some other social reinforcer.

A mand is also a by-product of many instances, in which the controlling variable is a state of deprivation or aversive stimulation. The mand *pull* evolved when responses having that form were reinforced when listeners pulled different things in different ways upon different occasions. It is possible that mands evolved first, and that they contributed to the evolution of tacts.

There are two types of mand. *Pull* is an action-mand, reinforced when the listener does something. *Fish*, as short for "Give me fish, please," is an object-mand, reinforced by the receipt of fish. An object-mand is more likely to occur in the presence of the object, because it has more often been reinforced in the presence of that object. We are much more likely to ask for the things we see in a shop because asking for presently available objects has more often been rein- forced. (That is one reason why shops exhibit their wares.) The control exerted by the stimulus in an object-mand does not make the response a tact as long as the reinforcing con- tingencies remain those of a mand—as long as saying "fish" is reinforced only by the receipt of a fish—but object-mands could have made some contribution to the evolution of a tact of the same form. (It does not follow that a speaker who says "fish" as a tact will therefore say it as an object-mand, or vice versa.)[3]

THE EVOLUTION OF AUTOCLITICS

If the occasion upon which a mand or tact has been reinforced recurs essentially unchanged, the behavior needs no further explanation. Reinforcement has had its usual effect. The crucial question is what happens when a person says something he or she has never said before. Novel behavior occurs on novel occasions, and an occasion is novel in the sense that its features have not appeared together before in the same arrangement. Some features of an occasion strengthen one response, others strengthen another. For example, if two people are walking together and one of them feels a few drops of rain, he may be inclined to say "Rain." The present listener or others like him have reacted to that response in reinforcing ways. He or others like him have also reacted in other ways to other features of a setting—when, for example, the speaker has shown surprise or disappointment. On this occasion the speaker may therefore say "Rain" in a surprised or disappointed tone of voice. Something has been added to the tact. It has been added to other responses in the past with reinforcing consequences, but never before to "Rain." The possibility of recombining the elements of vocal responses in this way accounts for much of the power and scope of verbal behavior.

Rather more important collateral effects on the listener bring us to the evolution of autoclitics, or—the traditional term—grammar. An important consideration for the listener is how effectively he can react to a tact-response. The speaker can help by indicating the nature and strength of the stimulus control of his behavior. If he has felt only a few drops of rain, he can speak in the tone of voice transcribed with a question mark: "Rain?" The listener is not to respond to the tact without reservation. Other elaborations of the response are needed

---

[3]See B. F. Skinner, *Verbal behavior* (New York: Appleton, 1957).

if the listener is either to respond as he would respond to rain itself or not to respond at all.

Responses that have such effects are "Yes" and "No." They often appear as mands having the effect of "Continue" and "Stop," respectively. Thus, we urge on a speaker who has paused by saying "Yes?" or stop him by saying "No!" Hearing "Rain? Yes!" a listener is more likely to act as if he had felt rain himself. Hearing "Rain? No!" he is less likely to do so. In traditional terms, the speaker asserts or denies the presence of rain.

A commoner alternative would be "It is raining" or "It is not raining." "Rain? Yes" and "Rain? No" do not have quite the same effect because they suggest questions and answers, but something of the thrust of "Yes" and "No" remains. The effect of "Yes" can be procured by emphasizing the word *is*. The speaker is saying, "You can safely act upon my response "'Rain.'" On the other hand, as a response that brings something the listener is doing to an end (as in saying "No" to someone about to go the wrong way), "No" is obviously close to *not*. "It is *not* raining" has the effect of "There are reasons why I tend to say 'Rain,' but do not act upon my response."

The steps through which particular autoclitics may have evolved are usually more obscure than the steps through which mands and tacts may have evolved. An early effort by John Horne Tooke in *The Diversions of Purley* (1786) has not been fully appreciated. That Tooke was not always right as an etymologist was not as important as his efforts to explain how English speakers could have come to say such words as *if, but,* and *and*. "We shall go tomorrow *given* it does not rain" is a clue to the origin of *if*. That the boy who stood on the burning deck should be *left out* in responding to "Whence all (be out him) had fled" is a clue to *but*. (That Mrs. Hemans wrote *all but he* instead of *all but him* is unfortunate but irrelevant.) And when we say *and*, we are often simply adding:

Of shoes-add ships-add sealing wax
Of cabbages—add kings

As we should put it today, autoclitics have evolved as instructions to the listener that help him behave in ways more likely to have reinforcing consequences and hence more likely to promote reciprocally reinforcing consequences for the speaker.

THE EVOLUTION OF SENTENCES

It is easy to understand the primitive view that behavior is inside the organism before it comes out. Perhaps there is a touch of the primitive in saying that behavior is "emitted," but we speak of the emission of light from a hot filament though the light is not in the filament. The reinforcement that strengthens a response does not put the response into the organism; it simply changes the organism so that it is more likely to respond in a given way. The point can be made by distinguishing between an operant as a probability of responding and a response as an instance. It is the operant that is "in" the organism, but only in the sense in which elasticity is "in" a rubber band.

What is reinforced in the sense of being followed by a given type of consequence is a response; it is the operant that is reinforced in the quite different sense of being strength-ened.[4] In the field of verbal behavior this distinction is close to that between the *sense* of what is said and the *saying* of it. The sense of a tact is the controlling variable—traditionally, what the tact means. The saying is an instance on a given occasion.

In traditional terms the distinction is close to that between *word* and *sentence*. *Sentence* comes from the Latin *sentire*, "to feel or think." We ask for a sentence when we say "How do you feel about that?" or "What do you think of that?" (A dictionary definition of a sentence is "a series of words that expresses a thought." That is an allusion, of course, to another kind of storage. We are said to possess thoughts and bring them out or "express: them by putting them into words.) As I have argued in *Verbal Behavior*, thinking can be adequately formulated simply as behaving. A sentence is not the expression of a thought; it *is* the thought. When we say, "It

---

[4]C. B. Ferster and I made that distinction in the glossary of our *Schedules of reinforcement* (New York: Appleton-Century, 1957).

occurred to me to look in my desk," we mean that the behavior of looking in the desk was strengthened, even if it was not executed. When we say, "The thought occurred to me that he was embarrassed," we mean that the verbal behavior "He is embarrassed" occurred to us, perhaps covertly. Looking in the desk is behavior; saying "He is embarrassed" is behavior. We are especially likely to call them thoughts when they are not overtly executed.

THE EVOLUTION OF FACTS

When we speak of the evolution of the automobile, we do not mean anything like the evolution of the horse. We mean the evolution of certain cultural practices through which new ways of making automobiles, as variations, were selected by their contributions to a reinforcing product of human behavior. Some products of verbal behavior may be treated in the same way. Facts, for example.

A fact is a statement about the world. When we say, "The fact of the matter is, I did not attend the meeting," we put the listener in the position of one who attended the meeting and observed that the speaker was not there. One who has been told "the facts of life" acts effectively in certain aspects of daily existence without passing through a series of instructional contingencies. Facts about what has happened in the past (the facts of history) can be helpful in this sense only to the extent that the conditions described are likely to recur. The facts of science are more helpful than those of history because the relevant conditions are repeated more often.

We may speak, then, of the evolution of facts—the facts of daily life, of history, or of science. Such facts are often called knowledge. At issue, however, is not the evolution of knowing or of knowledgeable persons, or of any organ of such a person, or of any condition of such an organ; at issue is a verbal environment or culture. People come into contact with such an environment when they listen to speakers or read books. The sounds they hear and the marks they see affect them as listeners or readers, just as the behavior of the original speakers or writers affected their listeners or readers.

We are said to know a fact either because we have already been changed by the contingencies or because we have been "told the fact." Thus, we say, "He must have known the door was unlocked; he would have tried it himself or someone would have told him." But there is also a sense in which we may "know" a fact simply as verbal behavior, whether or not it is acted upon. The behavior is *intraverbal*. The facts of history are examples.

There is an important difference between the intraverbals that result from contiguous usage (the *house-home* kind of thing) and the larger intraverbals that are learned as such (memorized historical facts or poetry, for example). By reciting facts as strings of intraverbal responses, we advise or inform ourselves, as the original speakers or writers advised or informed their listeners or readers.

COMMENTS

It is inevitable that a continuous process such as evolution should raise the question of boundaries. Systems for the classification of species are attempts to solve one problem of that kind. At what point can we say that human beings first appeared on earth? It may be useful to choose a given point to improve our use of the term *Homo sapiens*, but there was presumably no point at which an essence of humanity came into existence. Similarly, it is only for the sake of consistency that we should try to say when behavior first became verbal. Taking the fishing episode as an example, we could say that B's response became verbal (1) when it was first strengthened by A's action in pulling the net (that is, when it became a vocal operant); (2) when the same response was made in other settings with other consequences and came under the exclusive control of a fish as a discriminative stimulus, regardless of any particular state of deprivation or aversive stimulation (when it emerged as a tact); or (3) when it was shaped and maintained by a verbal environment transmitted from one generation to another (when it became part of a "language"). These are all distinguishable steps in the evolution of verbal behavior, and if we are to choose one of them, the most useful appears to be the third. Verbal behavior is behavior that is reinforced through the mediation of other people, but only when the other people are behaving in ways that have been shaped and maintained by an evolved verbal environment, or language. At level 3 we could say that other primates have engaged in verbal behavior in artificial verbal environments created by scientists but have not developed a language of their own.

LAUGHING AND CRYING

Two other functions of the vocal musculature—laughing and crying—are, if not exclusively human, at least highly characteristic of the species. There is a good chance that they evolved at about the same time as vocal behavior, but they are not operants, although they can be simulated as such—as in crying to get attention, for example, or laughing politely at an unfunny joke. As phylogenic behavior, they are elicited by positive and negative reinforcers, respectively; often the reinforcer is sudden. But if there is any immediate consequence for those who cry and laugh, it is obscure. Laughing and crying may have evolved because of their effects on others. There are those in whom signs of inflicted damage shape and maintain aggression, either nonverbal (a blow) or verbal (say, an insult), and there are those in whom signs of relief from damage shape helping others. Other species care for their young and for each other, but presumably not to any great extent as operant behavior. The human species may have gained important advantages when cessation of crying began to reinforce the behavior we call caring.

Laughing, on the other hand, quite obviously reinforces making people laugh, and making poeple laugh is associated with caring, since in general people laugh when things go well. Just as a courtship dance may have evolved because of its effects on other members of a species rather than upon the dancer, so laughing and crying may have evolved because of their effects on others rather than on those who laugh and cry.

TOPOGRAPHY

Theorists of the origin of language have often tried to explain form. Onomatopoeia, for example, has been said to explain why a dog is called a "bow-wow" and why bacon "sisses" or "sizzles" in the frying pan. The gesture for "Stop" is a kind of onomatopoeia, and Sir Richard Paget proposed that gesturing with the tongue may have modified the forms of uttered sounds in a useful way.[5] But onomatopoeia does not take us very far, and it may not be worthwhile to go further. Forms of words can be traced historically, but seldom back to their origins, and the languages of the world are so diverse that the sources must have been largely adventitious. Children invent new forms readily, and when two or more are living in relative isolation they may develop fairly extensive vocabularies. There is probably a reason for the form of every word, as there is probably a reason for the color of every bird or flower, but neither may be worth searching for as a particular fact.

When people began to describe the contingencies of reinforcement in the world around them, words could have been *invented* as the names of things. The sentence "That is called a rose" describes a contingency of reinforcement in a verbal environment. "Call that a rose" is advice to be followed if one is to behave successfully in such an environment. Children soon learn to ask for the names of things, as they ask for tools needed to do things, and it must have been a short step to the invention of a name ("Let's call that a rose"). The step is taken whenever parents name a child, although very often the form chosen has obvious sources.

CONCLUSION

To repeat a necessary caveat, I have not tried to say how a verbal environment, or the verbal behavior generated by such an environment, actually evolved. I have merely tried to say how it could have evolved, given the behavioral processes that

---

[5]R. A. Paget, *Human speech* (New York: 1930).

must already have been exhibited by the species. The chapter is speculative, but the speculation is under the restraint imposed by a commitment to the established principles of an operant analysis. In that respect it may be contrasted with the current approaches of linguists. A recent review of a book on essentially the present subject lists a number of explanatory principles or entities, among them "innate language organs," "mechanisms of speech perception," "grammatical competences," "cognitive neural substrates," and the "decoding and production functions of spoken language." It is doubtful whether any of them can be adequately defined without appeal to the observations they are said to explain, and they do not readily account for verbal behavior as such.

I have profited greatly from extensive discussions with Pere Julià concerning the position taken in this chapter.

chapter 7

Cognitive Science
and Behaviorism

꡷꡷꡷꡷꡷

Cognitive scientists are in no doubt about the importance of their field. A "Report of a Research Briefing Panel on Cognitive Science and Artificial Intelligence" claims that the questions to which it addresses itself "reflect a single underlying great scientific mystery, on a par with understanding the evolution of the universe, the origin of life, or the nature of elementary particles . . . ." The disciplines for which the panel speaks are "advancing our understanding of the nature of mind and the nature of intelligence on a scale that is proving revolutionary."[1]

The movement is called a revolution because it is said to have overthrown behaviorism. "Behaviorism," says Herbert Simon,

---

[1] W. K. Estes *et al.*, "Report of a research briefing panel on cognitive science and artificial intelligence," in *Research briefings 1983* (Washington, D.C.: National Academy Press, 1983), p. 19.

was suited to the predominantly positivist and operationalist views of the methodology and philosophy of science, and seemed to provide some guarantee against metaphysical, "mentalistic" explanations of human behavior. The price paid for these qualities was to confine experimental psychology to relatively simple memory and learning experiments, and to a preoccupation with laboratory rats rather than humans engaged in complex thinking and problem-solving tasks.[2]

The discipline that has replaced behaviorism, he says, shows a "new sophistication," a "new confidence," and a great gain in "precision and rigor." But what is cognitive science, what is behaviorism, and what is the difference between them?

The old mind-body problem is, of course, one issue. The Research Briefing Panel asked, "How can the brain give rise to all the phenomena that we call mental?" and "How can mind exist in a world totally controlled by physical laws?" A more important issue, however, is the origin of behavior. Cognitive science takes the traditional position: Behavior starts within the organism. We think and then act; we have ideas and then put them into words; we experience feelings and then express them; we intend, decide, and choose to act before acting. Behaviorists, in contrast, look at antecedent events in the environment and the environmental histories of both the species and the individual. The old stimulus-response formula was an attempt to give the environment an initiating role, but it has long been abandoned. The environment *selects* behavior. Ethologists study the species-specific behavior attributable to contingencies of survival in natural selection. Contingencies of operant reinforcement select the behavior of the individual in a similar way but, of course, on a very different time scale.

Cognitive scientists make the person an initiator when they adopt the paradigm of information processing. The adoption is apparently unanimous. As the Research Briefing Panel says, "Cognitive science and artificial intelligence stand together in taking information processing as the central activity involved in intelligent behavior . . . ." People have processed information, of course, for thousands of years. They

---

[2]Herbert Simon, "The behavioral and social sciences," *Science*, 209, 72 (1980), 76.

have made records of things that have happened—on clay tiles, papyrus, vellum, paper, magnetic tape, and now silicon chips—and they have stored them, retrieved them, and responded to them again more or less as they responded to the originals. Cognitive scientists have taken this practice as a model or metaphor. Are they justified in doing so?

PERCEPTION

The difference between the cognitive and behavioral approaches is perhaps best seen in the field of perception. For cognitive science the direction of action is from organism to environment. The perceiver acts upon the world, perceives it in the sense of taking it in. (*Perceive* comes from a Latin word meaning "capture.") This was an important point for Greek philosophers because to know was to be in contact with. The world had to be taken in and possessed in order to be known.

There is some ambiguity in calling perception the processing of information. Are sensory data the information to be processed, or is information extracted from them? In either case, processing must have a product, and for cognitive science that product is, as it was for the Greek philosopher, a *representation*. We do not see the world, we see copies of it.

In a behavioral analysis the direction is reversed. At issue is not what an organism sees but how stimuli alter the probability of its behavior. Stimuli acquire the power to do this from the part they play in contingencies of phylogenic and ontogenic selection. What is "seen" is a presentation, not a representation.

There is another step in the cognitive account. The perceiver must retrieve a stored history and in some way fuse it with a current representation. As one psychologist has put it; "Everyday perception involves assessing and bringing to bear vast stores of knowledge." In order to "make sense of the fragmentary pattern of light reaching the eye," one must consider many possibilities, make inferences, and formulate and test elaborate hypotheses.[3] A behavioral translation appeals only

---

[3]S. Sutherland, *Times Literary Supplement*, Sept. 1, 1978.

to the history of reinforcement responsible for the current effect of a presentation: Everyday perception is the product of a vast number of experiences in which fragmentary patterns of light, resembling those of the moment in many different ways, have been present when behavior has had many reinforcing consequences.

Cognitive psychologists also contend that the knowledge retrieved from storage affects not only what is seen but how readily it is seen. Thus, familiar words are seen more readily than rare words, "expected" words more readily than unexpected ones, and decorous words more readily than obscene ones. A behavioral account explains the same facts as the effects of past consequences, positive or negative. As the cognitive psychologist Donald Broadbent says, "nobody disputes the fact that the perception of a word would depend very much upon its probability of occurrence." But there is still a problem for the cognitive psychologist: "Why is it easier to perceive a word which is probable than a word which is improbable"?[4] The probability suffices in a behavioral account.

THE INNER MAN

A crucial difference between the two positions arises at the final stage. Once a representation has been constructed, what is done with it? The molecular biologist Gunther Stent has traced the processing of visual data, beginning with the roughly 100 million receptor cells in the retina and the roughly 1 million ganglion cells that, according to him, process the information coming from them by signaling light-dark contrasts and edge effects. The fibers of the ganglion cells connect the eye with the brain, where the "signals converge on a set of cortical nerve cells" that, among other things, process information from fields too big for the ganglion cells. For example, the "visual system of the frog abstracts its input data in such a way as to produce only two meaningful

---

[4]D. E. Broadbent, "Perceptual defence and the engineering psychologist," *Bulletin of the British Psychological Society*, 18 (1965), 1.

structures, 'my prey' and 'my predator,' which, in turn, evoke either of two alternative motor outputs, attack or flight."[5] (But why are "meaningful structures" needed? Why not simply "to produce only two alternative motor outputs"?) "It is not clear at present how far this process of cerebral abstraction by convergence of visual channels can be imagined to go," Stent concedes:

> Should one suppose that the cellular abstraction process goes so far that there exists for every meaningful structure of whose specific recognition a person is capable (for example, "my grandmother") at least one particular nerve cell in the brain that responds if and only if the light and dark pattern from which that structure is abstracted appears in its visual space?

The primrose path of the processing of information leads the cognitive scientist to a representation and the neurologist to a grandmother cell. But if what happens when one sees one's grandmother is the result of what has happened when one has seen her and persons like her many times in the past, changes must have taken place in most of the brain. A single cell is needed only in representing a putative "meaningful structure."

Stent concludes in a traditional way: "No matter how deeply we probe into the visual pathway, in the end we need to posit an 'inner man' who transforms the visual image into a percept." The Research Briefing Panel deals with this last stage rather more cavalierly: "The end-product of the analysis of a visual scene is subjectively familiar. We recognize the objects present in the environment and their spatial relations to each other and are able to compute distances in a way that permits us to navigate . . . ." Some cognitive touches survive in that statement: Apparently organisms cannot move about in the world without first "computing distances," and things they have seen before are only *subjectively* familiar, but "we" presumably means people, not little men in the brain, and "objects present in the environment" are presumably presentations and not representations. That is good behaviorism.

---

[5] G. S. Stent, *Science*, 187 (1975) 1056.

It is obviously not the whole organism that views a representation. It must be some lesser part inside. Cognitive science is forced to say so when it takes as a model the processing of information. In a behavioral account the whole organism responds, and it responds to the world around it—for reasons that an experimental analysis of behavior, with the help of neurology, will eventually discover.

RULES

Representations of sensory data are only one product of information processing. Another product plays a far more important role in cognitive science. Consider a familiar experiment: In an operant chamber a hungry rat occasionally presses a lever extending from one wall. When for the first time a bit of food is delivered after a single press, the rat eats and then presses the lever more rapidly. That is a simple fact, but cognitive psychologists want to say more about it. They want to say that "the rat has learned, and now *knows*, that pressing the lever brings food." "Pressing the lever brings food" tells us something about the apparatus. It is a description of the contingencies of reinforcement. In some form or other, say the cognitive psychologists, it passes into the head of the rat in the form of knowledge, a synonym of *cognition*. Processing has led not to a representation but to a rule.

There is no evidence that anything of the sort happens in a rat, but what about a person? Given the necessary exposure to a verbal community, a person could certainly say, "When I pressed the lever, food appeared," or, more generally, "When the lever is pressed, food appears." In that sense, people come to "know" the contingencies in the world around them. The behavior is verbal and must be analyzed as such.

Verbal behavior evidently came into existence when, through a critical step in the evolution of the human species, the vocal musculature became susceptible to operant conditioning. Processes shared with other species were already well established when that occurred, and they explain all the other features of verbal behavior.[6] A very large part of the social environment we call a culture consists of descriptions of contingencies of reinforcement in the form of advice, maxims, instructions, rules of conduct, the laws of governments and religions, and the laws of science. With their help, members of a group transmit what they have learned to new members, who then behave more effectively for one of two reasons: Their behavior is either directly shaped and maintained by contingencies of reinforcement, or it is controlled by descriptions of such contingencies. When we learn to drive a car, for example, we begin with responses to verbal stimuli. Our behavior is rule-governed. We flip switches, push pedals, and turn the wheel as we are told to do. But consequences follow and begin to shape and maintain our behavior. When we have become skillful drivers, the rules no longer function.

If contingencies are not adequate, we return to the rules. Most of the time, for example, we speak grammatically because of the prevailing contingencies in the verbal community, but when the contingencies are not sufficient, we turn to the rules of grammar. (An unnecessary return to rules may be troublesome. When the toad asked the centipede, "Pray, which leg goes after which?" the centipede "worked her mind to such a pitch/She lay distracted in the ditch/Considering how to run"—the victim of cognitive science.)[7]

Cognitive scientists argue that the rules are *in* the contingencies and that a person can learn about them in either way. They have therefore felt free to take the easier path and study rule-governed behavior. Settings are often merely described rather than presented; subjects are asked to imagine themselves in given situations and to say what they would do rather than to do it. Contingent consequences are suggested rather than imposed: "Assume that if you do A, B will follow." Yet everyone knows that descriptions of settings are never quite accurate or complete, that what people say they will do is not always what they actually do, and that a description of contingencies (for example, a statement of the odds in a

---

[6]B. F. Skinner, *Verbal behavior* (New York: Appleton-Century, 1957).
[7]Attributed to Mrs. Edmund Craster.

wager) seldom has the same effect as exposure to the contingencies (in repeated betting with those odds).

In an experiment on reaction time, for example, the subjects were said to have "understood that their task was to depress the response button as quickly as possible following the onset of the signal lights."[8] But how accurately does *understanding* describe the effect of a history of reinforcement, and how well are contingencies put into effect when an experimenter instructs subjects to respond "as quickly as possible"? Many years ago I arranged contingencies under which a pigeon pecked a key "as quickly as possible," and the reaction times were in the human range.[9] I do not believe one can learn from the cognitive literature how to do such an experiment. The response of which the reaction time is measured is quite different from the response of pulling the hand away from a painful stimulus, for example; to understand the difference (and give neurologists their proper assignment), one must specify the contingencies. Paying subjects according to their reaction times is a move in the right direction, but only a short one. Perhaps cognitive psychologists do not care why their subjects respond as quickly as possible; a measure of the speed of a cognitive process may be enough. But in the world at large, people behave as quickly as possible for reasons that need to be understood.

STORAGE

Are the contingencies of reinforcement to which a person is exposed stored as representations and rules, or is behavior simply changed by them? When physical records are stored, the records continue to exist until they are retrieved, but is that true when people "process information"? Would a storage battery not be a better model of a behaving organism? We put electricity into a battery and take it out when needed, *but there is no electricity in the battery*. When we "put electricity

---

[8]W. K. Estes, "Reinforcement in human behavior," *American Scientist* 60 (1972), 723.
[9]B. F. Skinner, "Are theories of learning necessary?" *Psychological Review*, 57 (1950), 193.

in," we *change* the battery, and it is a changed battery that "puts out electricity" when tapped. Organisms do not acquire behavior as a kind of possession; they simply change so that they behave in various ways. The behavior is not *in* them at any time. We say that it is emitted, but only as light is emitted from a hot filament: There is no light in the filament.

How organisms are changed by contingencies of reinforcement is the field of a behavioral analysis. What is happening inside is a question to be answered by neurology, with its appropriate instruments and methods. Cognitive scientists cannot leave this question to neurology because processing information is part of the story they want to tell. As the panel put it, a "prominent component of artificial intelligence systems is the memory organizations that hold the knowledge and permit finding the right bit of knowledge at the right time."

SURROGATES

Cognitive scientists presumably appeal to the storage and retrieval of representations and rules because they can then explain behavior by pointing to conditions that are present at the time the behavior occurs. The rat was changed when pressing the lever was reinforced, but it presses now "because it knows that pressing brings food." That knowledge is a current surrogate of the history of reinforcement. A classical example of a current surrogate is purpose. We say that we have eyes in order to see, but biologists have long since learned to say only that eyes have evolved because variations that enabled organisms to see better were selected. A similar mistake is made when cognitive psychologists call operant behavior purposive or goal-directed. The goal (in a maze, for example) has no effect upon the organism's behavior. Only past arrivals at the goal can have had any effect.

Cognitive psychologists need current surrogates of histories of selection in part because they pay little attention to selection as a causal principle. A new discipline, cognitive ethology, makes that mistake in an especially conspicuous way. Animals do many complex things: They use tools, lay traps, entice their victims. How can such behavior be explained? Ethologists answer by pointing to contingencies of survival in natural selection. Cognitive ethologists must do so too, to explain, for example, the gross anatomy of an organism (for which mental processes could scarcely be responsible), but they contend that some complex behavior cannot have evolved. Instead, what evolved must have been the structures that enable animals to have expectations and solve their problems by processing information. Behavior of comparable complexity can, however, be shaped if we arrange sequential contingencies of reinforcement, and these contingencies make it much easier to understand that contingencies of natural selection could have yielded the phylogenic instances.

Rationality

Expectation is a current surrogate of a history of reinforcement. It figures in recent studies of rationality. Herbert Simon calls the elucidation of the concept of rationality "[one] of the crowning achievements of the social sciences in the past two or three generations." "The core of the formal treatment of rationality," he says, "is the so-called subjective expected utility (SEU) theory." According to Simon, "human behavior is manifestly directed toward goals and the satisfaction of wants and needs." (In behavioral terms: People manifestly behave in ways that have had reinforcing consequences, the susceptibilities that make them reinforcing having arisen through natural selection or conditioning. "Wants" and "needs" are current surrogates of a history of deprivation.) "The rational actor is assumed to have a consistent preference ordering of all possible states of the world." (In behavioral terms: Reinforcers can be arranged according to their power to reinforce.) The axioms of SEU theory imply that "the actor maximizes his or her expected utility in the light of subjective estimates of the probabilities of events." (In behavioral terms: People act according to rules, possibly self-constructed, that describe or imply contingencies of reinforcement.) Missing from the cognitive account is any reference to the effect of the contingencies themselves, apart from the rules derived from them.

In a fairly typical experiment, two actions having probabilistic outcomes (for example, purchasing two kinds of lottery tickets) are described, and the subject is asked to choose between them. (As in much cognitive research, choice must be used because a more direct measure of probability of action is lacking.) The choice is then compared with what would be called rational in the light of the actual contingencies. But which ticket would the subject actually buy—either after the probabilities were first described to him (as rule-governed action) or after he had purchased many tickets and appropriate consequences had followed? To the extent that economic theory is concerned with what people *say* they will do, SEU theory may be adequate, but a behavioral scientist (and, one would suppose, an entrepreneur) must be concerned with what they actually do. People do those things most often that have been reinforced most abundantly, without making subjective estimates of the probabilities of reinforcement—and the reinforcers are real, not expected.

Because contingencies are usually more effective than the rules derived from them, we should not be surprised that, as Simon reports, "actual human choices depart radically from those implied by the axioms except in the simplest and most transparent of situations." This does not mean that people are "irrational" in the sense that contingencies of reinforcement are not effective. It means that descriptions of contingencies do not have the same effect as the contingencies themselves.

Feelings

Feelings are among the current surrogates of a history of reinforcement. According to cognitive psychologists, the rat not only learns and hence knows that pressing the lever brings food; it not only expects food to appear when it presses the lever; it *feels like* pressing the lever. A human subject would say as much. In a behavioral account, what one feels is one's body, and what one feels when one is behaving or likely to behave is therefore a collateral product of the causes of the behavior. The feeling should not be mistaken for a cause.

Cognitive psychologists sometimes challenge this position by asserting that feelings or states of mind cause other feelings or states of mind. Jerry Fodor, for instance, contends that

> mental causes typically give rise to behavioral effects by virtue of their interaction with other mental causes. For example, having a headache causes a disposition to take aspirin only if one also has the *desire* to get rid of the headache, the *belief* that aspirin exists, the *belief* that taking aspirin reduces headaches and so on. Since mental states interact in generating behavior, it will be necessary to find a construal of psychological explanations that posits mental processes: causal sequences of mental events. It is this construal that logical behaviorism fails to provide.[10]

But what is felt in each case can be "construed" as either a state of the behaving body or an external controlling variable, and it is *they* that interact.

Consider a simpler example. One pulls one's hand away from a hot object. Must one have a disposition to do so, a desire not to be burned, a belief that the hot object exists, and a belief that pulling the hand away will terminate the stimulus? Contingencies of survival in natural selection offer a much simpler explanation of that "flexion reflex." Contingencies of reinforcement offer a similar explanation of turning the steering wheel of a car to avoid a head-on collision. One need not have a belief in the existence of the oncoming car, a desire to avoid collisions, and a belief that turning the wheel will avoid one. Turning the wheel occurs because it has had fairly similar consequences in the past.

Neglected contingencies of reinforcement can be subtle. Kahneman and Tversky have reported that people say they would be less likely to buy a second ticket to the theater if a first had been lost than to buy a ticket after losing the money they had set aside for that purpose.[11] The difference, they say, is due to a difference in categorization. But a difference in relevant contingencies of reinforcement should not be over-

---

[10]J. A. Fodor, "The mind–body problem," *Scientific American*, 244 (1981), 116 (italics added).

[11]D. Kahneman and A. Tversky, *American Psychologist*, 39 (1984), 341.

looked. A girl who usually washes her hands before sitting down to dinner quite justly protests when told to wash them if she has already done so: "I *did* wash them!" We pay a bus fare and protest a subsequent request to do so again. Buying a ticket to the theater is in that "category" of contingencies. Contingencies that involve loss are different. We spoil one sheet of paper and take another. And, if not quite as readily, we use other money to buy a ticket to the theater.

THE BLACK BOX

In 1980 two writers argued in *American Psychologist* that "behaviorism . . . must accommodate itself to accepting the importance of what goes on inside the 'black box,' especially since we now have methods for *investigating its contents.*"[12] But what are those methods?

Introspection is presumably one of them. An early version of behaviorism (like logical positivism) held that science must confine itself to publicly observable events. But radical behaviorism accepts the argument that parts of our bodies enter into the sensory control of what we do, not only in behavior such as figure skating but in the self-observation and self-management that are shaped and maintained by a verbal community. But do we observe ourselves engaging in mental processes? Do we see ourselves extracting information from sensory data, or do we see merely the settings in which we are said to do so? Do we see ourselves storing and retrieving information or merely the "information" said to be stored and retrieved? We observe the conditions under which our behavior changes, and we observe the changed behavior, but do we see the changing? We have more information about ourselves than about other people, but it is only the same *kind* of information—about stimuli, responses, and consequences, some of them internal and in that sense private. We have no sensory nerves going to the parts of the brain that engage in "cognitive processes."

---

[12]H. Shevrin and S. Dickman, *American Psychologist*, 35 (1980), 421.

Brain science looks into the black box in another way. It has made great progress in discovering both the architecture and the chemistry of the brain, but what can it say about the processing of information? Visual representations are puzzling enough. What about *auditory* ones? Do we construct representations while listening to the *Emperor Concerto*, and how is the concerto stored in the head of the pianist who is playing it? A behavioral account is incomplete, in part because it leaves a great deal to neurology, but at least it avoids the problems of storage and retrieval. Cognitive psychologists, like psychoanalysts, observe causal relations between behavior and genetic and personal histories and invent mental apparatuses to explain them, but one may doubt that neurologists, with their very different and much more appropriate instruments and techniques of observation, will find anything like those apparatuses inside a person. In confining itself to the facts to which its instruments and methods are suited, behavioral science offers brain science a much more accurate statement of its assignment.

Simulation is said to be another source of information about the black box. Indeed, the Research Briefing Panel asserts that cognitive science and artificial intelligence stand together not only in taking information processing as the central activity involved in intelligent behavior but in "taking the framework of modern computer science as the foundation for understanding information processing systems." Apart from the advisability of using a framework as a foundation, are we to understand that the study of computers can tell us what we need to know about human behavior?

In constructing an artificial organism, that is, a system that exhibits artificial intelligence, one has a choice. One may simulate a nonverbal organism—say, a pigeon—and construct a sensorimotor system, the behavior of which is selected and strengthened by its consequences. Or one may construct a rule-following system that responds as directed and changes its behavior as directed. The first system would resemble a person who drives a car skillfully because of the way it behaves on the highway. One could study such a system by arranging various contingencies of reinforcement and observing the changes in its behavior that follow.

It is perhaps natural that those who are concerned with artificial intelligence should choose the second, rule-following alternative—resembling a man who drives a car by making only the moves he is told to make. That kind of artificial organism could be instructed to behave in intelligent ways, because specialists in artificial intelligence are intelligent, and could then be credited with intelligence.

The first system could, of course, learn to behave verbally, given the necessary verbal environment, and it would then resemble the second. The second, however, would remain forever simply a rule-following system. A computer may function as either type of system, but if cognitive scientists have actually programmed computers to "think creatively" and to make "scientific discoveries," they have simulated the first type. And in order to do so, they must have known a great deal more about it than cognitive science can tell them.

Linguistics is also said to have illuminated the black box, but most of linguistics is itself an offshoot of an earlier cognitive position. According to the Research Briefing Panel, speakers "learn to cope with language," acquire a vocabulary, and "[master] a complex of grammatical rules"; listeners possess a "natural language understanding system" with which they produce "internal representations of the information conveyed by the system" and make "a semantic analysis of the message conveyed by the language." That is a long way from throwing much light on what speakers and listeners actually do.

In a behavioral analysis, meaning is not *in* what speakers say; it is at best in the personal histories and current settings responsible for their saying it. Meaning for the listener is what the listener does as the result of a different personal history. Rules of grammar describe the contingencies maintained by verbal communities. Languages share "universals" because they serve universal functions. Speakers create settings in which listeners respond in given ways; nothing is communicated in the sense of being transmitted from one to the other. Sentences are "generated," but usually by contingencies of reinforcement and only occasionally with the help of rules extracted from them. Only when the contingencies are inadequate do speakers turn to rules.

The belief that meanings reside in words, that sentences have some kind of power, is hard to resist. A news commentator recently described the distressing problems some women face just before their period. "It is now known," he said, "that these problems are caused by the pre-menstrual syndrome." But the problems *are* the syndrome. Traditional doctors in a Moslem sect in Nigeria write an Islamic text on a slate, wash the slate with water, and give the water to their patients as medicine—a curious example of the processing of information and the communication of meaning.[13]

ACHIEVEMENT OR PROMISE?

One begins the report of that Research Briefing Panel with great expectations. The confidence and enthusiasm of the panel are typical of the field as a whole, but too many of its sections end with a mere promise. One subtheme is said to open "a research vista that is more than just the *hope of increased power*"; another is said to be merely "*pregnant with hope.*" One field is said to provide "a fund of knowledge about *possible* mechanisms upon which theories of human cognition can be built;" another "offers *promise* of a new burst of progress." Cognitive science is said to be able to "provide a broadened theoretical framework within which *significant progress* can occur . . . ." (italics added). Perhaps we should not ask more from a briefing panel, but what has actually been done that could or would not have been done if the information-processing revolution had never happened?

Step by step we may paraphrase the accomplishments of cognitive scientists in behavioral terms. They have not discovered "the form in which information is represented in images"; they have discovered some of the ways in which stimuli enter into the control of operant behavior. They have not discovered how "all intelligence . . . arises from the ability to use symbols"; at best they have learned something about verbal behavior. They have not studied rational choice; they have studied how people respond under conflicting con-

---

[13]A. Dickenson, *Bulletin of the British Psychological Society*, 33 (1980), 237.

tingencies of reinforcement or conflicting descriptions of contingencies. And so on. Many of them have made important discoveries and no doubt deserve credit even though they have misunderstood what they were doing. After all, we honor Columbus for discovering America, although he thought he was discovering India, and we are only now deciding not to call the original inhabitants of the continent Indians. Many of the findings of cognitive science find a useful place in behavioral analyses.

A TECHNOLOGY OF BEHAVIOR

The enthusiasm of cognitive scientists is not easily explained by looking at practical achievements. On the contrary, in reactivating the dream of the central initiating control of behavior, cognitive science has drawn attention away from the *accessible* variables needed in a technology.

The Research Briefing Panel's references to the teaching machines discussed in the following chapter are an example. The panel tells us that

> an intelligent tutoring system that can provide genuine help in educating a student in some well-understood domain, such as mathematics or science, must provide several components. (1) A powerful model of the task domain, so it can itself solve problems in that domain. (2) A detailed model of the student's current level of competence, encompassing both partial and erroneous competence as well as perfect competence. (3) Principles for interpreting the student's behavior, so as to be able to infer the student's knowledge and difficulties. (4) Principles for interacting with the student, so as to lead the student to a higher level of competence.

In many fewer words: To teach mathematics and science, we must (1) decide what we want our students to do, (2) find out what they can already do, (3) induce them to do more in carefully graded steps, and (4) tell them immediately when they have taken the steps successfully. Millions of students have suffered and millions more are now suffering from the difference between those versions—the first with its references to task domains, levels of competence, inferred knowledge, and principles of interaction, the second with its references to behavior and the contingencies of reinforcement of which behavior is a function.[14]

CONCLUSION

For many thousands of years, people have learned how to change the world and have told others what they have learned. In doing so they have talked about causes and effects. For at least three thousand of those years they have talked about human behavior in the same way, and for much of that time they have looked for causes inside the behaving organism. As Onians has shown, the Homeric Greek attributed much of human behavior to the *thumos* and the *phrenes*.[15] These words referred primarily to the heart and lungs but also to what we call feelings and states of mind. (In a rather similar way, many cognitive scientists use *brain* and *mind* interchangeably, as if the Greeks had simply chosen the wrong organ.) Plato and, much later, Descartes argued, of course, that there were two kinds of organs and that one could speak of feelings and states of mind without alluding to the body.

If what is felt are collateral products of the causes of behavior, then feelings can be a useful clue. We need a language of feelings and states of mind in our daily lives. Such is the language of literature and most of philosophy. Clinical psychologists use this language to learn many things about the histories of their clients which they could not discover in any other way. There are two languages in every field of knowledge, and it would be foolish to insist that the technical version always be used. But it must be used in *science*, and especially in a science of behavior.

Behaviorism began by asking philosophers and psychologists for definitions. What were sensations? What was con-

------

[14]See Chapter 8.

[15]R. D. Onians, *The origins of European thought* (Cambridge: Cambridge University Press, 1951).

sciousness? What were the dimensions of an idea? The effect was inhibiting, and people who wanted to talk more freely about human behavior were held in check. Cognitive science has opened the floodgates. The report of that Research Briefing Panel uses the following words, *all undefined*: intelligence, mind, mental operations, imagination, reasoning, induction, understanding, thinking, imagery, symbolic behavior, and intended meanings. Cognitive scientists are enjoying an intoxicating freedom, but we must ask whether it is a productive one.

The situation is serious, and perhaps a touch of rhetoric will be forgiven. I shall model my conclusion on Émile Zola's famous charge in the Dreyfus affair: "J'accuse . . . ."

I accuse cognitive scientists of misusing the metaphor of storage. The brain is not an encyclopedia, library, or museum. People are changed by their experiences; they do not store copies of them as representations or rules.

I accuse cognitive scientists of speculating about internal processes which they have no appropriate means of observing. Cognitive science is premature neurology.

I accuse cognitive scientists of emasculating laboratory research by substituting descriptions of settings for the settings themselves and reports of intentions and expectations for action.

I accuse cognitive scientists of reviving a theory in which feelings and states of mind observed through introspection are taken as the causes of behavior rather than as collateral effects of the causes.

I accuse cognitive scientists, as I would accuse psychoanalysts, of claiming to explore the depths of human behavior, of inventing explanatory systems that are admired for a profundity more properly called inaccessibility.

I accuse cognitive scientists of relaxing standards of definition and logical thinking and releasing a flood of speculation characteristic of metaphysics, literature, and daily intercourse, speculation perhaps suitable enough in such arenas but inimical to science.

Let us bring behaviorism back from the Devil's Island to which it was transported for a crime it never committed, and let psychology become once again a behavioral science.

chapter 8

The Shame
of American Education

୧ଈ୧ଈ୧ଈ୧ଈ୧ଈ

On a morning in October 1957, Americans were awakened by the beeping of a satellite. It was a Russian satellite, Sputnik. Why was it not American? Was something wrong with American education? Evidently so, and money was quickly voted to improve American schools. Now we are being awakened by the beepings of Japanese cars, radios, phonographs, and television sets, and again questions are being asked about American education, especially in science and mathematics.

Something does seem to be wrong. According to a report of the National Commission on Excellence in Education, for example, the average achievement of our high-school students on standardized tests is now lower than it was a quarter of a century ago, and students in American schools compare poorly with those in other nations in many fields.[1] As the commission put it, America is threatened by "a rising tide of mediocrity."

---

[1] National Commission on Excellence in Education, *A nation at risk: The imperative for educational reform* (Washington, D.C.: U.S. Department of Education, 1983).

The first wave of reform is usually rhetorical. To improve education, it is said, we need "imaginative innovations," a "broad national effort" leading to a "deep and lasting change," and a "commitment to excellence." More specific suggestions have been made, however. To get better teachers we should pay them more, possibly according to merit. They should be certified to teach the subjects they teach. To get better students, scholarship standards should be raised. The school day should be extended from six to seven hours, more time should be spent on homework, and the school year should be lengthened from 180 to 200 or even 220 days. We should change what we are teaching. Social studies are all very well, but they should not take time away from basics, especially mathematics.

As many of us have learned to expect, there is a curious omission in that list: It contains no suggestion that teaching be improved. There is a conspiracy of silence about teaching as a skill. The *New York Times* publishes a quarterly survey of education. Three such surveys from the early 1980s[2] contained eighteen articles about the kinds of things being taught in schools; eleven articles about the financial problems of students and schools; ten articles about the needs of special students, from the gifted to the disadvantaged; and smaller numbers of articles about the selection of students, professional problems of teachers, and sports and other extracurricular activities. Of about seventy articles, only two had anything to do with how students are taught or how they could be taught better. Pedagogy is a dirty word.

TIME LAGS

In January 1981, Frederick Mosteller, president of the American Association for the Advancement of Science, gave an address called "Innovation and Evaluation."[3] He began with an example of the time that can pass between a scientific discovery and its practical use. That lemon juice cures scurvy was discovered in 1601, but more than 190 years passed

---

[2]For November 14, 1982, January 9, 1983, and April 24, 1983.
[3]F. Mosteller, "Innovation and evaluation," *Science*, 211 (1981), 881–86.

before the British navy began to use citrus juice on a regular basis and another 70 before scurvy was wiped out in the mercantile marine—a lag of 264 years. Lags have grown shorter, but as Mosteller pointed out they are often still too long. Perhaps unwittingly he gave another example. He called for initiatives in science and engineering education and said that a major theme of the 1982 meeting of the association would be a "national commitment to educational excellence in science and engineering for all Americans."

When Mosteller's address was published in *Science*, I wrote a letter to the editor[4] calling attention to an experiment in teaching algebra in a school in Roanoke, Virginia.[5] In this experiment an eighth-grade class using simple teaching machines and hastily composed instructional programs went through all of ninth-grade algebra in *half* a year. Their grades met ninth-grade norms, and when tested a year later the students remembered rather more than usual. Had American educators decided that that was the way to teach algebra? They had not. The experiment was done in 1960, but education had not yet made any use of it. The lag was already twenty-one years.

A month or so later I ran into Mosteller. "Did you see my letter in *Science* about teaching machines?" I asked. "Teaching machines?" he said, puzzled, "Oh, you mean *computers—* teaching machines to *you*." And, of course, he was right. *Computer* is the current word. But is it the right one? Computers are now badly misnamed. They were designed to compute, but they are not computing when they are processing words, or displaying Pac-Man, or aiding instruction (unless the instruction is in computing). *Computer* has all the respectability of the white-collar, but let us call things by their right names. Instruction may be *computer-aided*, and all good instruction must be *interactive*, but machines that teach are teaching machines.

I liked the Roanoke experiment because it confirmed something I had said a few years earlier to the effect that with

---

[4]B. F. Skinner, "Innovation in science teaching." *Science*, 212 (1982), 283.

[5]E. W. Rushton, *The Roanoke experiment* (Chicago: Encyclopedia Britannica Press, 1965).

teaching machines and programmed instruction one could teach what is now taught in American schools in half the time with half the effort. I shall not review other evidence that that is true. Instead I shall demonstrate my faith in a technology of teaching by going out on a limb. I claim that the school system of any large American city could be so redesigned, at little or no additional cost, that students would come to school and apply themselves to their work with a minimum of coercion and, with very rare exceptions, learn to read with reasonable ease, express themselves well in speech and writing, and solve a fair range of mathematical problems. I want to talk about why this has not been done.

The teaching machines of twenty-five years ago were crude, of course, but that is scarcely an explanation. The calculating machines were crude too, yet they were used until they could be replaced by something better. The hardware problem has now been solved, but resistance to a technology of teaching survives. The rank commercialism that quickly engulfed the field of teaching machines is another possible explanation. Too many people rushed in, wrote bad programs, and made promises that could not be kept. But that should not have concealed the value of programmed instruction for so many years. There is more to be said for the marketplace in the selection of a better mousetrap.

PSYCHOLOGICAL ROADBLOCKS

I shall argue that educators have not seized this chance to solve their problems because the solution conflicts with deeply entrenched views of human behavior, and that these views are too strongly supported by current psychology. Humanistic psychologists, for example, feel threatened by any kind of scientific analysis of human behavior, particularly if it leads to a "technology" that can be used to intervene in people's lives. A technology of teaching is especially threatening. Carl Rogers has said that teaching is vastly overrated, and Ivan Illich has called for the de-schooling of society. I dealt with the problem in *Beyond Freedom and Dignity*.[6] For example, we do not like to be told something we already know; we can then no longer claim credit for having known it.

To solve that problem, Plato tried to show that students already possess knowledge and have only to be shown that they possess it. But the famous scene in Plato's *Meno* in which Socrates shows that the slave boy already knows Pythagoras's theorem for doubling the square is one of the great intellectual hoaxes of all time. The slave boy agrees with everything Socrates says, but there is no evidence whatsoever that he could then go through the proof by himself. Indeed, Socrates says that the boy would need to be taken through it many times before he could do so.

Cognitive psychology is causing much more trouble, but in a different way. It is hard to be precise because the field is usually presented in what we may call a cognitive style. For example, a pamphlet of the National Institute of Education quotes with approval that "at the present time, modern cognitive psychology is the dominant theoretical force in psychological science as opposed to the first half of the century when behavioristic, anti-mentalistic stimulus-response theories of learning were in the ascendance" (the writer means "ascendant").[7] The pamphlet tells us that cognitive science studies learning, but not in quite those words. Instead, cognitive science is said to be "characterized by a concern with understanding the mechanisms by which human beings carry out complex intellectual activities including learning." The pamphlet also says that cognitive science can help construct tests that will tell us more about what a student has learned and hence how to teach better, but here is the way it says this: "Attention will be placed on two specific topics: Applications of cognitive models of the knowledge structure of various subject matters and of learning and problem solving to construction of tests that identify processes underlying test answers, analyze errors, and provide information about what

---

[6]B. F. Skinner, *Beyond freedom and dignity* (New York: Knopf, 1971).

[7]National Institute of Education, "Science and technology and education," in *The five-year outlook: Problems, opportunities and constraints in science and technology*, Vol. 2 (Washington, D.C.: National Science Foundation, 1980), p. 391.

students know and don't know, and strategies for integrating testing information with instructional decisions." Notice especially the cognitive style in the last phrase—the question is not "whether test results can suggest better ways of teaching" but "whether there are strategies for integrating testing information with instructional decisions."

The Commission on Behavioral and Social Sciences and Education of the National Research Council provides another example in its announcement of a biennial program plan covering the period 1 May 1983 to 30 April 1985. The commission will take advantage of "significant advances . . . in the cognitive sciences."[8] Will it study learning? Well, not exactly. The members will "direct their attention to studies of fundamental processes underlying the nature and development of learning." Why do cognitive psychologists not tell us frankly what they are up to? Is it possible that they themselves do not really know?

Cognitive psychology is certainly in the ascendant. The word *cognitive* is sprinkled through the psychological literature like salt—and, like salt, not so much for any flavor of its own as to bring out the flavor of other things, things that would have been called by other names a quarter of a century ago. The heading of an article in a recent issue of the APA *Monitor* tells us that "cognitive deficits" are important in understanding alcoholism.[9] In the text we learn simply that alcoholics show losses in perception and motor skills. Perception and motor skills used to be fields of psychology; now they are fields of cognitive science. Nothing has been changed except the name, and the change has been made for suspicious reasons. There is a sense of profundity about "cognitive deficits," but it does not take us any deeper into the subject.

Much of the vogue of cognitive science is due to advances in computer technology. The computer offers an appealing simplification of some old psychological problems. Sensation and perception are reduced to input; learning and memory to

[8]National Research Council, Commission on Behavioral and Social Sciences and Education, *Biennial program plan, May 1, 1983–April 30, 1985* (Washington D.C.: National Academy Press, 1984), p. 41.

[9]C. Turkington, "Cognitive deficits hold promise for prediction of alcoholism," *APA Monitor*, June 1983, p. 16.

the processing, storage, and retrieval of information; and action to output. It is very much like the old stimulus–response formula patched up with intervening variables. To say that students process information is to use a doubtful metaphor, and how they process information is still the old question of how they learn.

Cognitive psychology also gains prestige from its alignment with brain research. Interesting things are certainly being discovered about the biochemistry and circuitry of the brain. But we are still a long way from knowing what is happening in the brain as behavior is shaped and maintained by contingencies of reinforcement, and that means we are a long way from help in designing useful instructional practices.

Cognitive science is also said to be supported by modern linguistics, a topic to which I am particularly sensitive. Programmed instruction emerged from my analysis of verbal behavior,[10] which linguists, particularly generative grammarians, have, of course, attacked. So far as I know, they have offered no equally effective practices. One might expect them to have improved the teaching of languages, but almost all language laboratories still work in outmoded ways; language instruction is one of the principal failures of precollege education.

Psycholinguistics moves in essentially the same direction in its hopeless commitment to development. Behavior is said to change in ways determined by its structure. The change may be a function of age, but age is not a variable that one can manipulate. The extent to which developmentalism has encouraged a neglect of more useful ways of changing behavior is shown by a recent report in which the number of studies concerned with the development of behavior in children was found to have skyrocketed, whereas the number concerned with how children learn had dropped so low that the researcher could find scarcely any examples at all.[11]

There are many cognitive psychologists who are doing fine research, but they are not the cognitive psychologists who

---

[10]B. F. Skinner, *Verbal behavior* (New York: Appleton-Century, 1957).

[11]R. S. Siegler, "Five generalizations about cognitive development," *The American Psychologist*, 38 (1983), 263–77.

for twenty-five years have been promising great advances in education. A short paper published in *Science* in April 1983 asserts that "recent findings in cognitive science suggest new approaches to teaching in science and mathematics."[12] The examples given, however, when expressed in noncognitive style, are simply these: (1) Students learn about the world in "naive" ways before they study science; (2) naive theories interfere with learning scientific theories; (3) we should therefore teach science as early as possible; (4) many problems are not solved exclusively with mathematics; qualitative experience is important; (5) students learn more than isolated facts; they learn how facts are related to each other; and (6) students relate what they are learning to what they already know. If these are *recent* findings, where has cognitive science been?

Cognitive psychology is frequently presented as a revolt against behaviorism, but it is not a revolt, it is a retreat. Everyday English is full of terms derived from ancient explanations of human behavior. We spoke that language when we were young. When we went out into the world and became psychologists, we learned to speak in other ways but made mistakes for which we were punished. But now we can relax. Cognitive psychology is Old Home Week. We are back among friends speaking the language we spoke when we were growing up. We can talk about love and will and ideas and memories and feelings and states of mind, and no one will ask us what we mean; no one will raise an eyebrow.

SCHOOLS OF EDUCATION

Psychological theories come into the hands of teachers through schools of education and teachers' colleges, and it is there, I think, that we must lay the major blame for what is happening in American education. In a recent article in the *New York Times Magazine*, President Leon Botstein of Bard College proposed that schools of education, teachers' colleges,

---

[12]L. B. Resnick, "Mathematics and science learning: A new conception," *Science*, 220 (1983), 477.

and departments of education simply be disbanded. But he gave a different reason. He said that schools of that sort "placed too great an emphasis on pedagogical techniques and psychological studies."[13] Instead, he argued, they should have been teaching the subjects the teachers will eventually teach. But disbanding such schools is certainly a move in the wrong direction. It has long been said that college teaching is the only profession for which there is no professional training. Would-be doctors go to medical schools, would-be lawyers go to law schools, and would-be engineers go to institutes of technology, but would-be college teachers just start teaching. Fortunately it is recognized that grade- and high-school teachers need to learn to teach. The trouble is, they are not being taught in effective ways. The commitment to humanistic and cognitive psychology is only part of the problem.

Equally damaging is the assumption that teaching can be adequately discussed in everyday English. The appeal to laymanship is attractive. At the Convocation on Science and Mathematics in the Schools called by the National Academies of Sciences and Engineering, one member said that "what we need are bright, energetic, dedicated young people, trained in mathematics . . . science . . . or technology, mixing it up with 6- to 13-year-old kids in the classroom."[14] The problem is too grave to be solved in any such way. The first page of the report notes with approval that "if there is one American enterprise that is local in its design and control it is education." That is held to be a virtue. But certainly the commission would not approve similar statements about medicine, law, or science and technology. Why should the community decide how children are to be taught? The commission is actually pointing to one explanation of why education is failing.

We must beware the fallacy of the good teacher and the good student. There are many good teachers who have not needed to learn to teach. They would be good at almost anything they tried. There are many good students who scarcely need to be taught. Put a good teacher and a good student

---

[13]L. Botstein, "Nine proposals to improve our schools," *New York Times Magazine*, June 5, 1983, p. 64.

[14]S. Raizen, *Science and mathematics in the schools: Report of a convocation* (Washington, D.C.: National Academy Press, 1983).

together and you have what seems to be an ideal instructional setting. But it is disastrous to take it as a model to be followed in our schools, where hundreds of thousands of teachers must teach millions of students. Teachers must learn how to teach, and they must be taught by schools of education. They need only to be taught more effective ways of teaching.

A SOLUTION

We could solve our major problems in education if students learned more during each day in school. That does not mean a longer day or year or more homework. It simply means using time more efficiently. Such a solution is not considered in any of the reports I have mentioned—whether from the National Institute of Education, the American Association for the Advancement of Science, the National Research Council, or the National Academies of Sciences and Engineering. Nevertheless, it is within easy reach. Here is all that needs to be done.

1. Be clear about what is to be taught. When I once explained to a group of grade-school teachers how I would teach children to spell words, one of them said, "Yes, but can you teach spelling?" For him, students spelled words correctly not because they had learned to do so but because they had acquired a special ability. When I told a physicist colleague about the Roanoke experiment in teaching algebra, he said, "Yes, but did they learn algebra?" For him, algebra was more than solving certain kinds of problems; it was a mental faculty. The more words you learn to spell, the easier it is to spell new words, and the more problems you solve in algebra the easier it is to solve new problems. What eventually emerges is often called *intuition*. We do not know what it is, but we can certainly say that no teacher has ever taught it directly, nor has any student ever displayed it without first learning to do the kinds of things it supposedly replaces.

2. Teach first things first. It is tempting to move too quickly to final products. I once asked a leader of the "new math" what he wanted students to be able to do. He was rather puzzled and then said, "I suppose I just want them to be

able to follow a logical line of reasoning." That does not tell a teacher where to start or, indeed, how to proceed at any point. I once asked a colleague what he wanted his students to do as a result of having taken his introductory course in physics. "Well," he said, "I guess I've never thought about it that way." I'm afraid he spoke for most of the profession.

Among the ultimate but useless goals of education is "excellence." A candidate for president recently said that he would let local communities decide what that meant. "I am not going to try to define excellence for them," he said, and wisely so. Another useless ultimate goal is "creativity." It is said that students should do more than what they have been taught to do. They should be creative. But does it help to say that they must acquire creativity? More than 300 years ago, Molière wrote a famous line: "I am asked by the learned doctors for the cause and reason why opium puts one to sleep, to which I reply that there is in it a soporific virtue, the nature of which is to lull the senses." Several years ago an article in *Science* pointed out that 90 percent of scientific innovations were accomplished by fewer than 10 percent of scientists. The explanation, it was said, was that only a few scientists possess creativity. Molière's audiences laughed. Eventually some students behave in creative ways, but they must have something to be creative with and that must be taught first. Then they can be taught to multiply the variations that give rise to new and interesting forms of behavior. (Creativity, incidentally, is often said to be beyond a science of behavior, and it *would* be if that science were a matter of stimulus and response. By emphasizing the selective action of consequences, however, the experimental analysis of behavior deals with the creation of behavior precisely as Darwin dealt with the creation of species.)

3. Stop making all students advance at essentially the same rate. The phalanx was a great military invention, but it has long been out of date, and it should be out of date in American schools. Students are still expected to move from kindergarten through high school in twelve years, and we all know what is wrong: Those who could move faster are held back, and those who need more time fall farther and farther behind. We could double the efficiency of education with one

change alone—by letting each student move at his or her own pace. (I wish I could blame this costly mistake on developmental psychology, because it is such a beautiful example of its major principle, but the timing is out of joint.)

No teacher can teach a class of thirty or forty students and allow each to progress at an optimal speed. Tracking is too feeble a remedy. We must turn to individual instruments for part of the school curriculum. The report of the convocation held by the National Academies of Sciences and Engineering refers to "new technologies" that can be used to extend the educational process, to supplement the teacher's role in new and imaginative ways," but that is scarcely an enthusiastic endorsement of technology. Thirty years ago educational television was promising, but the promise has not been kept. The report alludes to "computer-aided instruction" but calls it the latest "rage of education" and insists that "the primary use of the computer is for drill." (Properly programmed instruction is *never* drill if that means going over material again and again until it is learned.) The report also contains a timid allusion to "low-cost teaching stations that can be controlled by the learner," but evidently these stations are merely to give the student access to video material rather then to programs.

4. Program the subject matter. The heart of the teaching machine, call it what you will, is the programming of instruction—an advance not mentioned in any of the reports I have cited. Standard texts are designed to be read by the students, who will then discuss what they say with a teacher or take a test to see how much has been learned. Material prepared for individual study is different. It first induces students to say or do the things they are to learn to say or do. Their behavior is thus "primed" in the sense of being brought out for the first time. Until the behavior has acquired more strength, it may need to be prompted. Primes and prompts must then be carefully "vanished" until the behavior occurs without help. At that point the reinforcing consequences of being right are most effective in building and sustaining an enduring repertoire.

Working through a program is really a process of discovery, but not in the sense in which that word is currently used in education. We discover many things in the world around us, and that is usually better than being told about them, but as individuals, we can discover only a very small part of the world. Mathematics has been discovered very slowly and painfully over thousands of years. Students discover it as they go through a program, but not in the sense of doing something for the first time in history. Trying to teach mathematics or science as if the students themselves were discovering things for the first time is not an efficient way of teaching the very skills with which, in the long run, a student may, with luck, actually make a genuine discovery.

When students move through well-contructed programs at their own pace, the so-called problem of motivation is automatically solved. For thousands of years students have studied to avoid the consequences of not studying. Punitive sanctions still survive, disguised in various ways, but the world is changing, and they are no longer easily imposed. The great mistake of progressive education was to try to replace them with natural curiosity. Teachers were to bring the real world into the classroom to arouse the students' interest. The inevitable result was a neglect of subjects in which children were seldom naturally interested—in particular, the so-called basics. One solution is to make some of the natural reinforcers—goods or privileges—artificially contingent upon basic behavior, as in a token economy. Such contingencies can be justified if they correct a lethargic or disordered classroom, but there should be no lethargy or disorder. It is characteristic of the human species that successful action is automatically reinforced. The fascination of video games is adequate proof. What would industrialists not give to see their workers as absorbed in their work as young people in a video arcade? What would teachers not give to see their students applying themselves with the same eagerness? (For that matter, what would any of us not give to see ourselves as much in love with our work?) But there is no mystery; it is all a matter of the scheduling of reinforcements.

A good program of instruction guarantees a great deal of successful action. Students do not need to have a natural interest in what they are doing, and subject matters do not need to be dressed up to attract attention. No one really cares whether Pac-Man gobbles up all those little spots on the screen. As soon as the screen is cleared, the player covers it again with little spots to be gobbled up. What is reinforcing is successful play, and in a well-designed instructional program, students gobble up their assignments. I saw them doing that when I visited the project in Roanoke. The director, Allen Calvin, and I entered a room in which thirty or forty eighth-grade students were at their desks using rather crude teaching machines. When I said I was surprised that they paid no attention to us, Calvin proposed a better demonstration. He asked me to keep my eye on the students. He went up to the teacher's platform, jumped in the air, and came down with a loud bang. Not a single student looked up. Students do not have to be made to study. Reinforcement is enough, and good programming provides it.

THE TEACHER

Individually programmed instruction has much to offer teachers and makes very few demands upon them. Paraprofessionals may take over some of their chores. That is not a reflection on teachers or a threat to their profession. There is much that only teachers can do, and they can do it as soon as they have been freed of unnecessary tasks.

Some things they can do are talk to and listen to students and read what students write. A recent study found that teachers are responding to things that students say during only 5 percent of the school day.[15] If that is so, it is not surprising that one of the strongest complaints against our schools is that students do not learn to express themselves.

If given a chance, teachers can also be interesting and sympathetic companions. It is a difficult assignment in a classroom in which order is maintained by punitive sanctions. The word *discipline* has come a long way from its association with *disciple* as one who understands.

Success and progress are the very stuff on which programmed instruction feeds. They should also be the stuff that

---

[15]J. L. Goodlad, *A place called school* (New York: McGraw-Hill, 1983).

makes teaching worthwhile as a profession. Just as students must not only learn but know that they are learning, so teachers must not only teach but know that they are teaching. Burnout is usually regarded as the result of abusive treatment by students, but it can be as much the results of looking back upon a day in the classroom and wondering what one has accomplished.

THE ESTABLISHMENT

The effect of a technology of teaching on the educational establishment may be much more disturbing. More than fifty years ago Sidney Pressey invented a simple teaching machine and predicted the coming "industrial revolution" in education. In 1960 he wrote to me, "Before long the question will need to be faced as to what the student is to do with the time which automation will save him. More education in the same place or earlier completion of full-time education?"[16] Earlier completion is a problem. If what is now taught in the first and second grades can be taught in the first (and I am sure that it can), what will the second-grade teacher do? What is now done by the third- or fourth-grade teacher? At what age will the average student reach high school, and at what age will the student graduate? Certainly a better solution is to teach more effectively what is now taught and to teach many other things as well. Even so, students will probably reach college younger in years. But they will be more mature, and that change will more than pay for the inconvenience of making sweeping administrative changes.

The report of the National Commission on Excellence in Education repeatedly mistakes causes for effects. It says that "the educational foundations of our society are being eroded by a rising tide of mediocrity," but is the mediocrity causing the erosion? Should we say that the foundations of our automobile industry are being eroded by a rising tide of mediocre cars? Mediocrity is an effect, not a cause. Our educational foundations are being eroded by a commitment to laymanship

---

[16]Sidney Pressey, letter to author, 1960.

and to theories of human behavior that simply do not lead to effective teaching. The report of the Convocation on Science and Mathematics in the Schools quotes President Reagan as saying that "this country was built on American respect for education . . . . Our challenge now is to create a resurgence of that thirst for education that typifies our nation's history." But is education in trouble because it is no longer held in respect, or is it not held in respect because it is in trouble? Is it in trouble because people do not thirst for education, or because they do not thirst for what is being offered?

Everyone is unhappy about education, but what is wrong? Let us look at a series of questions and answers rather like the series of propositions that logicians call a *sorites*:

1. Are students at fault when they do not learn? No, they have not been well taught.
2. Are teachers then at fault? No, they have not been properly taught to teach.
3. Are schools of education and teachers' colleges then at fault? No, they have not been given a theory of behavior that leads to effective teaching.
4. Are behavioral scientists then at fault? No, a culture too strongly committed to the view that a technology of behavior is a threat to freedom and dignity is not supporting the right behavioral science.
5. Is our culture then at fault? But what is the next step?

Let us review the sorites again and ask what can be done. Shall we:

1. Punish students who do not learn by flunking them?
2. Punish teachers who do not teach well by discharging them?
3. Punish schools of education that do not teach teaching well by disbanding them?
4. Punish behavioral science by refusing to support it?
5. Punish the culture that refuses to support behavioral science?

But you cannot punish a culture. A culture is punished by its failure or by other cultures that take its place in a continually evolving process. There could scarcely be a better example of the point of my book *Beyond Freedom and Dignity*.

A culture that is not willing to accept scientific advances in the understanding of human behavior, together with the technology that emerges from these advances, will eventually be replaced by a culture that is.

When the National Commission on Excellence in Education said that "the essential raw materials needed to reform our educational system are waiting to be mobilized," it spoke more truly than it knew, but to mobilize them the commission called for "leadership." That is as vague a word as excellence. Who, indeed, will make the changes that must be made if education is to play its proper role in American life? It is reasonable to turn to those who suffer most from the present situation.

1. Those who pay for education—primarily taxpayers and the parents of children in private schools—can simply demand their money's worth.
2. Those who use the products of grade- and high-school education—colleges and universities on the one hand and business and industry on the other—cannot refuse to buy, but they can be more discriminating.
3. Those who teach may simply withdraw from the profession, and too many are already exercising their right to do so. The organized withdrawal represented by a strike is usually a demand for higher wages, but it could also be a demand for better instructional facilities and administrative changes that would improve classroom practices.

But why must we always speak of higher standards for students, merit pay for teachers, and other versions of punitive sanctions? These are the things one thinks of first, and they will no doubt make teachers and students work harder, but they will not necessarily have a better effect. They are more likely to lead to further defection. There is a better way: Give students and teachers better reasons for learning and teaching. That is where the behavioral sciences can make a contribution. They can develop instructional practices so effective and so attractive in other ways that no one—student, teacher, or administrator—will need to be coerced into using them.

Young people are by far the most important natural resource of a nation, and the development of that resource is assigned to education. Each of us is born needing to learn what others have learned before us, and much of it needs to be taught. We would all be better off if education played a far more important part in transmitting our culture. Not only would that make for a stronger America (remember Sputnik), but we might also look forward to the day when the same issues could be discussed about the world as a whole—when, for example, all people produce the goods they consume and behave well toward each other, not because they are forced to do so but because they have been taught something of the ultimate advantages of a rich and peaceful world.

chapter 9

How to Discover What You Have to Say: A Talk to Students

ຂໍ ຂໍ ຂໍ ຂໍ ຂໍ ຂໍ ຂໍ

My title will serve as an outline. It begins with "How to," and this is a "How to" talk. It is about a problem we all face, and the solution I propose is an example of verbal self-management, an example that uses my *Verbal Behavior* as the basis of a technology.[1] At issue is how we can manage our own verbal behavior more effectively. (I may note in passing that psycholinguistics, a very different kind of analysis, largely structural and developmental, has given rise to no comparable technology, in part because it so often devotes itself to the listener rather than the speaker.)

Verbal behavior begins almost always in spoken form. Even when we write, we usually speak first, either overtly or covertly. What goes down on paper is then a kind of self-dictation. I am concerned here only with written behavior and even so with only a special kind, the kind of writing at the heart of a paper, a thesis, or a book in a field such as the analysis of behavior. What such writing is "about" is hard to say—indeed, that is just the problem. Certain complex cir-

---

[1] B. F. Skinner, *Verbal Behavior* (New York: Appleton-Century, 1957).

cumstances call for verbal action. You have a sheet of paper and a pen: What happens next? How do you arrive at the best possible account?

Do I mean how are you to "think" about those circumstances, to "have ideas" about them? Yes, if those terms are properly defined. In the last chapter of *Verbal Behavior*, I argue that thinking is simply behaving, and it may not be too misleading to say that verbal responses do not express ideas but are the ideas themselves. They are what "occur to us" as we consider a set of circumstances. If I have forgotten the key to my house and "it occurs to me" to look under the mat, it is not an idea that has occurred to me but rather the behavior of looking, and it occurs because under similar circumstances I have found a key under the mat or have heard someone say, "The key is under the mat." What verbal responses "express" are not preverbal ideas but the past history and present circumstances of the speaker. But how are we to arrive at the most effective expression? How can we behave verbally in a way that is most relevant to a problem at hand?

It is hard to give a "how to" talk without posing as an authority. I hasten to say that I know that I could write better than I do, but I also know that I could write worse. Over the years I believe I have analyzed my verbal behavior to my advantage. What distresses me is that I should have done so so late. Possibly some of what I have learned may help you at an earlier age.

"DISCOVER"

The next key word in my title is "discover." If that word suggests that verbal behavior lurks inside us waiting to be uncovered, it is a bad term. We do not really "search our memory" for forgotten names. Verbal behavior, like all behavior, is not inside the speaker or writer before it appears.

A first step is to put yourself in the best possible condition for behaving verbally. La Mettrie thought that he had supporting evidence for his contention that men were machines. He could not think clearly when he was ill. (Freud, on the other hand, said that he could write only when experiencing a certain discomfort.) Certainly many writers have testified to the importance of diet, exercise, and rest. Descartes, one of the heroes of psychology, said that he slept ten hours every night and "never employed more than a few hours a year at those thoughts which engage the understanding . . . I have consecrated all the rest of my life to relaxation and rest." Good physical condition is relevant to all kinds of effective behavior but particularly to that subtle form we call verbal.

Imagine that you are to play a piano concerto tomorrow night with a symphony orchestra. What will you do between now and then? You will get to bed early for a good night's rest. Tomorrow morning you may practice a little but not too much. During the day you will eat lightly, take a nap, and in other ways try to put yourself in the best possible condition for your performance in the evening.

Thinking effectively about a complex set of circumstances is more demanding than playing a piano, yet how often do you prepare yourself to do so in a similar way? Too often you sit down to think after everything else has been done. You are encouraged to do this by the cognitive metaphor of thinking as the expression of ideas. The ideas are there; the writer is simply a reporter.

What about drugs? Alcohol? Tobacco? Marijuana? There are authentic cases of their productive effects in poetry and fiction, but very few in which they have had a good effect on serious thinking. Tacitus said that the Germans made their decisions when drunk but acted upon them when sober, and Herodotus said the same of the Persians. In other words, it may be possible to solve an intellectual problem when drunk or stoned, but only if the solution is reviewed soberly. In spite of much talk of expanded consciousness, good examples of work produced with the help of drugs are still lacking.

So much for the condition of your body. Equally important are the conditions in which the behavior occurs. A convenient place is important. It should have all the facilities needed for the execution of writing: pens, typewriters, recorders, files, books, a comfortable desk and chair. It should be a pleasant place and should smell good. Your clothing should be comfortable. Since the place is to take control of a particular kind of behavior, you should do nothing else there at any time.

It is helpful to write always at the same time of day. Scheduled obligations often raise problems, but an hour or two can almost always be found in the early morning—when the telephone never rings and no one knocks at the door. And it is important that you write something, regardless of quantity, every day. As the Romans put it, *Nulla dies sine linea*— No day without a line. (They were speaking of lines drawn by artists, but the rule applies as well to the writer.)

As a result of all this, the setting almost automatically evokes verbal behavior. No warm-up is needed. A circadian rhythm develops that is extremely powerful. At a certain time every day, you will be highly disposed to engage in serious verbal behavior. You will find evidence of this when traveling to other time zones, when a strong tendency to engage in serious verbal behavior appears at the usual time, though it is now a different time by the clock.

It may be a mistake to try to do too much at first. Such a situation only slowly acquires control. It is enough to begin with short sessions, perhaps fifteen minutes a day. And do not look for instant quality. Stendhal once remarked, "If when I was young I had been willing to talk about wanting to be a writer, some sensible person might have said to me: 'Write for two hours every day, genius or not.' That would have saved ten years of my life, stupidly wasted in waiting to become a genius."

How should you spend the rest of the day? Usually you will have little choice, for other demands must be met. But there is usually some leisure time, and a fundamental rule is not to try to do more writing. You may tease out a few more words, but you will pay the price the next morning. The Greeks spoke of *eutrapelia*—the productive use of leisure. A little experimentation will reveal the kinds of diversion that maximize your subsequent productivity.

There is an exception to the rule against writing away from your desk. Verbal behavior may occur to you at other times of day, and it is important to put it down in lasting form. A notebook or a pocket recorder is a kind of portable study. Something you see, hear, or read sets off something relevant, and you must catch it on the wing. Jotting down a brief reminder to develop the point later is seldom enough, because the conditions under which it occurred to you are the best conditions for writing a further account. A longer note written at the time will often develop into something that would be lost if the writing were postponed. The first thing that occurs to you may not be the most important response in a given situation, and writing a note gives other verbal behavior a chance to emerge.

As notes accumulate they can be classified and rearranged, and they will supply some of the most important materials for your papers or books. One of the most widely reprinted and translated papers of mine, "Freedom and the Control of Men,"[2] was first written almost entirely in the form of notes. When I was asked for a paper on that theme, I found that it was practically written. Notes left over can of course be published in a notebook, as I have recently found.[3] The metaphor of discovery redeems itself at this point. When you have constructed the best possible conditions for the production of verbal behavior and have provided for catching occasional verbal responses on the wing, you are often *surprised* by what turns up. There is no way you can see all of your verbal behavior before you emit it.

I am not talking about how to *find* something to say. The easiest way to do that is to collect experiences, as by moving about in the world and by reading and listening to what others say. A college education is largely a process of collecting in that sense. And so, of course, is exploration, research, or a full exposure to daily life. Nor am I talking about the production of ideas through the permutations and combinations of other material. A very different kind of idea is generated, for example, by playing with contradictions or antinomies. The young Marx was addicted: "The world's becoming philosophical is at the same time philosophy's becoming worldly, . . ." "That the rational is real is proved even in the contradiction of irrational reality that is at all points the opposite of what it proclaims, and proclaims the opposite of what it is." "History

---

[2]B. F. Skinner, "Freedom and the control of men," *American Scholar*, Winter 1955–56.
[3]B. F. Skinner, *Notebooks* (Englewood Cliffs, N.J.: Prentice-Hall, 1980).

has long enough been resolved into superstition, but now we can resolve superstition into history." I daresay Marx thought he was discovering something worth saying, and the verbal play suggests profundity, but it is a dangerous practice.

"YOU"

The next key word is "You." Who is the you who has something to say? You are, of course, a member of the human species, absolutely unique genetically unless you have an identical twin. You also have a personal history that is absolutely unique. Your identity depends upon the coherence of that history. More than one history in one lifetime leads to multiple selves, no one of which can be said to be the real you. The writer of fiction profits from the multiplicity of selves in the invention of character.

We also display different selves when we are fresh or fatigued, loving or angry, and so on. But it is still meaningful to ask what *you* have to say about a given topic *as an individual*. The you that you discover is the you that exists over a period of time. By reviewing what you have already written, going over notes, reworking a manuscript, you keep your verbal behavior fresh in your history (not in your mind!), and you are then most likely to say all that you have to say with respect to a given situation or topic. Obviously, it will not be simply what you have read or heard. It is easy to get books out of the books of other people, but they will not be your books.

"HAVE TO SAY" I

The last three key words of my title are "Have to Say," and they have at least three meanings. The first is the verbal behavior I have just identified—the thing we refer to when we ask a person "What do you have to say to that?" We are simply asking "What is your verbal behavior with respect to that?"

"HAVE TO SAY" II

A second meaning is what you *have* to say in the sense of *must* say. It is usually easy to distinguish between the things we want to do and those we have to do to avoid the consequences of not doing them, where *have to* refers to aversive control. A familiar example is the pause in conversation that must be filled and that leads, too often, to verbal behavior about trivia—the weather, the latest news, what someone is wearing. It is also the occasion for hasty and ungrammatical speech, or nonsense, or revealing slips. We feel much the same aversive pressure when, say, we prematurely exhaust our notes during an hour lecture. It is then that we tend to borrow the verbal behavior of others and resort to clichés and phrases or sentences that simply stall for time ("It is interesting to note that . . . ." "Let us now turn to . . . .").

The results are not always bad. Many famous writers have worked mostly under aversive pressure. Balzac wrote only when he needed money, Dostoevski only in return for advances he had received. Aversive control may keep you at work, but what you write will be traceable to other variables if it is any good. Moreover, it is under such conditions that writers report that writing is hell, and if you write primarily to avoid the consequences of not writing, you may find it hard to resist other forms of escape—stopping to get a cup of coffee, needlessly rereading something already written, sharpening pencils, calling it a day.

There may be an aversive element in maintaining the schedule that builds a circadian rhythm. It is not always easy to get up at five o'clock in the morning and start writing. Even though you make the space in which you work so attractive that it reinforces your behavior in going to it, some aversive control may be needed. But other variables must take over if anything worthwhile is to be written. Positive reinforcement may be as irresistible as negative, and it is more likely to lead you to say effectively what you have to say.

The great generalized reinforcer, money, is usually poorly contingent upon behavior at your desk. It controls too effectively when a writer begins to write only the kinds of things that have sold well. Prestige and fame are also long-deferred consequences inadequately contingent upon the production of sentences. But progress toward the completion of a book that may lead to money or prestige and fame may help, if the progress is made clear. Some kind of record of the number of words or pages you write may act as a reinforcing consequence. For years, an electric clock on my desk ran only when the light was on, and I added a point to a cumulative record whenever the clock completed twelve hours. The slope of the curve showed me how much time I was spending each day (and how damaging it was to go off on a speaking tour!). A simple calculation reinforces that reinforcer. Suppose you are at your desk two hours a day and produce on the average 50 words an hour. That is not much, but it is about 35,000 words a year, and a book every two or three years. I have found this to be reinforcing enough.

Other immediate consequences are more effective in discovering what you have to say. Saying something for the first time that surprises you, clearing up a confusing point, enjoying what you have written as you read it over—these are the things that in the long run are the most likely to produce verbal behavior that is your own. The best reason for liking what you have written is that it says what you have to say.

An audience as a source of reinforcers is not to be overlooked. As Pascal put it, "There are those who speak well and write badly. The occasion, the audience fires them and draws from them more than they find in themselves without this heat." Writing often suffers when it is not directed toward a particular kind of reader. Just as in writing a letter to a close friend you may find a picture helpful, or at least a warm salutation at the head of the letter, so some visible sign of an audience may help. Reading what someone else has said about you sometimes strengthens behavior, since one is seldom at a loss for words in a warm discussion. I once used E. G. Boring's *The Physical Dimensions of Consciousness*[4] as an instrument of self-management. I disagreed so violently with the author's position that after reading a page or two I would find my verbal behavior very strong. And one day when I was lecturing to a class but was not speaking well, I noticed that a

---

[4]E. G. Boring, *Physical dimensions of consciousness* (New York: Century, 1933).

student had brought his parents. My behavior changed dramatically under the influence of that new audience. Searching for good audiences may be worthwhile.

Just as those who write for money may begin to write things that sell rather than write what they have to say as individuals, so an audience may have too strong an effect. I once gave what was supposed to be the same lecture to fifteen audiences. I used a good many slides that served as an outline, but I began to abbreviate or drop comments that did not seem to arouse interest and retain everything that brought a clean-cut response or a laugh. Near the end of the series, I had to struggle to say anything worthwhile.

That verbal behavior is sustained by the prevailing contingencies is clear from the fact that writing shows many effects of scheduling. Fixed-ratio reinforcement often produces a "snowball effect": The closer one comes to finishing a piece of work, the easier it is to work on it (where *easy* means that one works without moving to escape or without "forcing oneself" to remain at work). Writing papers, articles, or stories one after the other "for a living" tends to be on a ratio schedule, and the "post reinforcement pause" takes the form of abulia, or "not being able to get started on something new."

There are many reasons why you may stop writing or "find it difficult" to go on. When something is not going well, when you are not saying anything important, when matters remain as confusing as ever, extinction sets in. You may continue, but only because aversive consequences take over. Punishment in the form of frequent criticism decreases production, a point not recognized by teachers of composition who spend most of their time pointing to the faults in their students' work.[5]

Satiation also weakens behavior. Many novelists never tell a story before they write it. Just as you cannot tell the same story to the same company a second time (or at least with the same effect!), so you are less likely to get a novel written if you have already told the plot. Enforced silence is a

---

[5]J. S. Vargas, "A behavioral approach to the teaching of composition," *Behavior Analyst*, 1 (1978), 16–24.

useful practice. Satiation also sets in when one writes more or less to the same effect again and again.

There is also a kind of subject-matter fatigue. One starts to write in excellent condition but eventually becomes "sick of the subject." One solution is to work on two subjects at the same time. It is easier to write short sections of two papers during a session than to spend the whole session on one.

"HAVE TO SAY" III

A third sense of "have to say" is the heart of the matter. In a paper called "On 'Having' a Poem,"[6] I compared a poet to a mother. Although the mother bears the child and we call it her child, she is not responsible for any of its features. She gave it half its genes, but she got those from her parents. I argued that the same thing could be said of the poet. Critics who trace the origins and influences of a poem seem to agree, at least to the extent that they can account for features of a poem by pointing to the verbal or nonverbal history of the poet. Samuel Butler's comment that "A hen is simply an egg's way of making another egg" holds for the human egg as well and for the poet. A poet is a literary tradition's way of making more of a literary tradition. (Much the same thing could be said of the scholar. A psychologist is just psychology's way of making more psychology.)

But the mother does make a contribution: She nourishes, protects, and in the end gives birth to the baby, and so does the poet and so does the scholar. There is a process of verbal gestation. Your history as a writer lacks the structure and coherence of the behavior that eventually emerges from it. Sentences and paragraphs are not lurking inside you waiting to be born. You possess some behavior in the form of prefabricated sentences, and may often do little more than utter them as such, possibly with minor changes, but that is not discovering what you have to say.

---

[6]B. F. Skinner, "On 'having' a poem," *Saturday Review,* July 15, 1972. Reprinted in *Cumulative Record* (New York: Appleton-Century-Crofts, 1972).

A new situation may strengthen dozens—possibly hundreds—of verbal responses that have never before been strengthened together at the same time. They may lack organization. Relations among them may be unclear. They will have little effect on the reader who has not had the same history and is not confronted by the same situation. They must therefore be ordered and interrelated in an effective way. That is what you do as you compose sentences, paragraphs, and at last a book. Only then will your verbal behavior lead to successful action on the part of your reader or to a less active but still behavioral "understanding" of what you are saying.

Verbal Behavior takes up these stages in order. The first half of the book describes the kinds of verbal operants produced by different contingencies of reinforcement. Although these are more than structures, because they have probabilities of reinforcement, they are not assertions. The second half describes how these operants are fashioned into effective verbal discourse as they are asserted, qualified, denied, and so on, in such a way that the reader responds effectively. The writer thus generates sentences as effective sequences of the material emerging upon a given occasion.

I have found the following rules helpful in discovering what one has to say in this sense.

Rule 1. Stay out of prose as long as possible. The verbal behavior evoked by the setting you are writing about does not yet exist in the form of sentences, and if you start by composing sentences, much will be irrelevant to the final product. By composing too early you introduce a certain amount of trash that must later be thrown away. The important parts of what you have to say are manipulated more easily if they have not yet become parts of sentences.

Rule 2. Indicate valid relations among responses by constructing an outline. Very large sheets of paper (say, 22 by 34) are helpful. Your final verbal product (sentence, paragraph, chapter, book) must be linear—with a bit of branching—but the variables contributing to your behavior are arranged in many dimensions. Numbering the parts of a composition decimally is helpful in making cross-references and temporary indexes and in noting connections among parts. As bits of verbal behavior are moved about, valid arrangements will appear and sentences will begin to emerge. It is then time to "go into prose."

Rule 3. Construct the first prose draft without looking too closely at style. "Full speed ahead, and damn the stylebook." (How hard that will be depends upon the extent to which aversive control has been used in teaching you to write.) When what you have to say about a given state of affairs exists at last in prose, rewrite as you please, removing unnecessary words, articulating sentences with better connectives, rearranging as seems necessary, and so on. At this stage, some advice on style is helpful. I read Follett's *Modern American Usage*[7] straight through every two or three years.

There is an old distinction between ecstatic and euplastic composition. There have been times when ecstatic verbal behavior (impulsive, unreasoned) was particularly admired, because it seemed more genuine, less contrived. In poetry and some forms of fiction it may be particularly effective. But in writing about a complex subject matter, it is too much to expect that adequate statements will appear fully formed. Neither phylogenically nor ontogenically has verbal behavior evolved to the point at which a complex combination of personal history and a current situation will give rise to a passage having an appropriate effect upon the reader. Only the most skillful euplastic (reasoned) management of verbal behavior will suffice.

CONCLUSION

Possibly I am confessing some special need for crutches. No doubt other people arrive more quickly at effective statements. They do not need to work as hard to say important things. I myself did not need to work as hard when I was younger. I am simply telling you how I succeed in saying what I have to say. Of course I wish I had had more to say and that I had said it better, and I wish I could tell you more clearly what I have learned about saying it, but it would be impossi-

---

[7]Wilson Follett, *Modern American Usage* (New York: 1966).

ble to tell you all you need to know. No two people are alike; your personal histories will lead you to respond in different ways. You will have to work out your own rules. As in any application of a behavioral analysis, the secret of successful verbal self-management is understanding what verbal behavior is all about.

chapter 10

Intellectual Self-Management in Old Age

 za za za za za za

More than a quarter of a century ago I presented a paper at the Eastern Psychological Association meeting called "A Case History in Scientific Method." In it I pointed out that my life as a behavioral scientist did not seem to conform to the picture usually painted by statisticians and scientific methodologists. The present chapter is also a case history, but in a very different field. I have heard it said that G. Stanley Hall, one of the founding fathers of psychology, wrote a book on each of the stages of his life as he passed through it. I did not have the foresight to begin early enough to do that, but I can still talk about the last stage and so I now present myself to you behaving verbally in old age as I once presented those pigeons playing Ping-Pong.

Developmentalism is a branch of structuralism in which the form, or topography, of behavior is studied as a function of time. At issue is how behavior changes as one grows older. *Aging* should be the right word for this process, but it does not mean developing. In accepted usage, *to develop* is not simply to grow older but to unfold a latent structure, to realize an inner potential, to become more effective. *Aging*, on the other hand, usually means growing less effective. For Shakespeare the "ages of man" ranged from the infant mewling and puking, to the schoolboy "creeping like snail unwillingly to school," to lovers sighing and soldiers seeking the bubble reputation, to the justice full of wise saws and modern instances, to a stage in which the "big manly voice . . . pipes and whistles in his sound," and then at last to second childishness and mere oblivion—"sans teeth, sans eyes, sans taste," and in the end, of course, "sans everything." The aged are old people. Aging is growing not merely older but old.

In developmentalism the horticultural metaphor is strong. There are stages of *growth*, and *maturity* is hailed as a desirable state of completion. But then the metaphor becomes less attractive, for there is a point at which we are glad to stop developing. Beyond maturity lie decay and rot. Fortunately, the developmental account is incomplete, and what is missing is particularly important if we want to do anything about aging. There is, no doubt, an inexorable biological process, a continuation of the growth of the embryo, which can be hindered or helped but not stopped. When we speak of the development of an *organism*, growth is no metaphor, but *persons* develop in a different way and for different reasons, many of which are not inexorable. Much of what seems to be the unfolding of an inner potential is the product of an unfolding environment: A person's *world* develops. The aging of a person, as distinct from the aging of an organism, depends upon changes in the physical and social environments. We recognize the difference when we say that some young people are old for their years or when, as Shakespeare put it, old people return to childishness. Fortunately, the course of a developing environment can be changed, That kind of aging can be retarded.

If the stages in our lives were due merely to the passage of time, we should have to find a fountain of youth to reverse the direction of change, but if many of the problems of old people are due to shortcomings in their environments, the environments can be improved.

Organism and person do not, of course, develop independently; the biological changes interact with the environmental contingencies. As the senses grow dull, the stimulating environment becomes less clear. As muscles grow slower and weaker, fewer things can be done successfully. Changes in sensory and motor capacities are conspicuous in games and other forms of competition, and athletes retire young just because of aging.

Many remedial steps are, of course, well known. Eyeglasses compensate for poor vision and hearing aids for poor hearing. These are conspicuous prosthetic devices, but what is needed is a *prosthetic environment* in which, in spite of reduced biological capacities, behavior will be relatively free of aversive consequences and abundantly reinforced. New repertoires may be needed as well as new sources of stimulation, If you cannot read, listen to book recordings. If you do not hear well, turn up the volume on your phonograph (and wear headphones to protect your neighbors). Foods can be flavored for aging palates. Paul Tillich, the theologian, defended pornography on the ground that it extended sexuality into old age. And there is always the possibility, secondhand though it may be, of living the highly reinforcing lives of others through literature, spectator sports, the theater and movies, and television.

There is nothing particularly new in all this, but there is a special problem to which little attention has, I think, been given. One of the inexorable effects of biological aging is particularly important for those engaged in intellectual work—in writing, inventing, composing, painting, having ideas—in a word, thinking. It is characteristic of old people not to think clearly, coherently, logically, or in particular, creatively. In physiological terms we should have to say that deterioration occurs not only in sense organs and effectors but in central processes. The changes are certainly central if we are talking about the nervous system, but changes in behavior are changes in the body as a whole.

Forgetting is a classical problem. It is most conspicuous in forgetting names because names have so little going for them by way of context. I have convinced myself that names are very seldom wholly forgotten. When I have time—and I mean something on the order of half an hour—I can almost always recall a name if I have already recalled the occasion for using it. I work with thematic and formal prompts, in the latter case going through the alphabet, testing for the initial letter. But that will not work in introducing your wife to someone whose name you have forgotten. My wife and I use the following strategy: If there is any conceivable chance that she could have met the person, I simply say to her, "Of course, you remember . . . ?" and she grasps the outstretched hand and says, "Yes, of course. How are you?" The acquaintance may not remember meeting my wife, but he is not sure of his memory either.

The failure to produce a name at the right moment, as in making an introduction, can be especially punishing, and the punishment is part of the problem. Stutterers are all the more likely to stutter because they have failed to speak fluently in the past, and an emotional state called "anxiety" has been conditioned. Similarly, we may fail to recall a name when making an introduction in part because of past failings. We are, as we say, afraid we are going to forget. Some help may come from making such situations as free from aversive consequences as possible. Graceful ways of explaining your failure may help. Appeal to your age. Flatter your listener by saying that you have noticed that the more important the person, the easier it is to forget the name. Recall the amusing story about forgetting your own name when you were asked for it by a clerk. If you are skillful at that sort of thing, forgetting may even be a pleasure. Unfortunately, there is no similar strategy when you are suffering from a diminished access to verbal behavior while writing a paper. Nevertheless, a calm acceptance of deficiencies and a more careful observance of good intellectual self-management may have a comparable effect.

The problem is raised by the way in which we make use of past experience, the effects of which seem to fade too quickly. A special set of techniques is needed for its solution, Practical examples may be helpful before turning to comparable intellectual behavior.

Ten minutes before you leave your house for the day you hear a weather report: It will probably rain before you return. It occurs to you to take an umbrella (the sentence means quite literally what it says: the behavior of taking an umbrella occurs to you), but you are not yet able to do so. Ten minutes later you leave without the umbrella. You can solve that kind of problem by executing as much of the behavior as possible when it occurs to you. Hang the umbrella on the doorknob, or put it through the handle of your briefcase, or in some other way start the process of taking it with you.

Here is a similar intellectual problem: In the middle of the night it occurs to you that you can clarify a passage in the paper you are writing by making a certain change. At your desk the next day you forget to make the change. Again, the solution is to make the change when it occurs to you, using, say, a notepad or tape recorder kept beside your bed. The problem in old age is not so much how to have ideas as how to have them when you can use them. A written or dictated record, consulted from time to time, has the same effect as the umbrella hung on the doorknob. A pocket notebook or recorder helps to maximize one's intellectual output by recording one's behavior when it occurs. The practice is helpful at any age, but particularly so for the aging scholar. In place of memories, memorandums.

Another symptom of the same failing is to forget what you were going to say. In a conversation you wait politely until someone else finishes, and your own clever comment has then vanished. One solution is to keep saying it to yourself; another is to appeal to the privilege of old age and interrupt the speaker; another is to make a note (perhaps pretending it is about what the other person is saying). The same problem arises when *you* are speaking and digress. You finish the digression and cannot remember why you embarked on it or where you were when you did so. The solution is simply not to digress—that is, not to interrupt yourself. A long sentence always raises that kind of problem: The last part is not likely to agree with the first because the first has passed out of reach. The effect is especially common if you are speaking a language you do not speak well. In that case it is always a mistake to embark upon complex sentences. You will do much better if you speak only simple sentences, and the same remedy is available to the aging scholar who is giving an impromptu address in his or her own language. Short sentences are also advisable when you are talking to yourself—in other words, when you are thinking.

A different kind of problem is solved by skillful prompting. You are going to attend a class reunion and are taking someone with you whom you must introduce to old friends. How can you remember their names? Before you go, look in your alumni register for a list of those who will be there, visualizing them if you can. The textual stimuli will prompt names that must otherwise be emitted, if at all, simply in response to the appearances of your friends.

Forgetting a name is only a conspicuous example of the essential failing. In writing a paper or thinking about a problem, there are relevant responses that would occur sooner or in greater abundance to a younger person. Their absence is not as conspicuous as a forgotten name, but it must be acknowledged and dealt with. One way to increase the probability that relevant responses will occur while you are writing a paper or solving a problem is to read relevant material and reread what you have written. Reference books within easy reach will supply prompts for names, dates, and other kinds of information. A thesaurus can be used, not to find a new word, but to prompt an old one. It is possible to prepare yourself even for extemporaneous speaking. You may "put yourself in better possession" of the verbal behavior you will be emitting by rehearsing your speech just one more time.

Old age is like fatigue, except that its effects cannot be corrected by relaxing or taking a vacation. Particularly troublesome is old age *plus* fatigue, and half of that can be avoided. It may be necessary to be content with fewer good working hours per day, and it is particularly necessary to spend the rest of the time in what the Greeks called *eutrapelia*—the productive use of leisure. Leisure should be relaxing. Possibly you like complicated puzzles, or chess, or other intellectual games. Give them up. If you want to continue to be intellectually productive, you must risk the contempt of your younger acquaintances and freely admit that you read detective stories or watch Archie Bunker on television.

The kind of fatigue that causes trouble has been called mental, perhaps because it has so little to do with the physical fatigue of labor. You can be fully rested in a physical sense yet tired of what you are doing intellectually. To take appropriate steps one needs some way to measure fatigue. Curiously enough, Adolf Hitler can be of help. In a report to the Nieman Foundation, William Lederer has called attention to relevant documents in the Harvard library. Toward the end of the Second World War, Hitler asked the few social scientists left in Germany to find out why people made bad decisions. When they reported that it was when they were mentally exhausted, he asked them for a list of the signs of mental fatigue. Then he issued an order: Any officer showing signs of mental fatigue should immediately be sent on vacation. Fortunately for the world, he did not apply the order to himself.

Among the signs on Hitler's list are several I find helpful. One is an unusual use of profanity or blasphemy. According to that principle, at least two of our recent presidents must have been mentally exhausted. When I find myself saying "damn," I know it is time to relax. (That mild expletive is a sign of my age as well as of my fatigue; I have never felt right about the scatological language of young people.) Other signs on Hitler's list include an inclination to blame others for mistakes, procrastinating on making decisions, an inclination to work longer hours than normally, an inclination to feel sorry for oneself, a reluctance to take exercise and relax, and dietary extremes—either gluttonous appetite or almost none at all. Clues not on Hitler's list that I have found useful are especially bad handwriting and mistakes in playing the piano.

Effects on my thinking are much harder to spot, but I have learned to watch for a few of them. One is verbal padding. The ancient troubador sang or spoke standard lines that gave him time to remember what to say next. Phrases like "At this point it is interesting to note . . . ." or "Let us now turn to another aspect of the problem . . ." serve the same function. They hold the floor until you have found something to say. Fatigued verbal behavior is also full of clichés, inexact descriptions, poorly composed sentences, borrowed sentences, memorized quotations, and Shakespeare's "wise saws." These are the easy things to say and they come out when you are tired. They can be avoided, if at all, only by avoiding fatigue.

I could have doubled my readership by calling this article "Cognitive Self-Management in Old Age." *Cognitive* means so many things that it could scarcely fail to apply here. But I could have described the field much more accurately by speaking of *verbal* self-management, because the problems are primarily verbal. We have a repertoire of verbal behavior, every item of which presumably has a resting probability of "occurring to us." As a layperson might put it, there are lots of ideas waiting to be had. Some of them have occurred many times, are strengthened by common features of our daily life, and hence are the ideas that it is easiest to have as we think about or write about a problem. But they generally yield hackneyed, shopworn stuff. What is worth saying—the idea that is possibly unique to us because of the uniqueness of our experience and hence more likely to be called original— is least likely to occur. In short, in old age special difficulties arise because verbal behavior becomes less and less accessible. Perhaps we can do nothing about the accessibility, but we can improve the conditions under which behavior occurs.

It helps to make behavior as easy as possible. There are no crutches or wheelchairs for the verbally handicapped, but some prosthetic support is available—convenient pens, pencils, and paper, a good typewriter (a word processor, if possible), dictating equipment, and a convenient filing system.

I find it harder to "think big thoughts" in the sense of moving easily from one part of a paragraph to another or from one part of a chapter to another. The intraverbal connections are weak, and inconsistencies are therefore likely. The prosthetic remedy is to use outlines—spatial arrangements of the materials of a paragraph, chapter, or book. Decimal notation is helpful, with successive digits indicating chapter, section, paragraph, and sentence, in that order. This may look like constraint, but it is constraint against senile nattering, inconsistencies, and repetition. You remain free to change an outline as a paragraph or chapter develops. An index, constructed as you write, will help you answer questions such as "Now where did I take *that* up?" or "Have I already said that?"

It is commonly believed that those who have passed their prime can have nothing new to say. Jorge Luis Borges exclaimed, "What can I do at 71 except plagiarize myself!" Among the easiest things to say are things that have already been said, either by others or, especially, by ourselves. What we have already said most closely resembles what we now have to say. One of the more disheartening experiences of old age is discovering that a point you have just made—so significant, so beautifully expressed—was made in something you published a long time ago.

But one *can* say something new. Creative verbal behavior is not produced by exercising creativity; it is produced by skillful self-management. The creation of behavior raises the same issues as the creation of species. It is a selective process, and the appearance of something new—the *origin* in Darwin's title—can be promoted by the introduction of variations. You are also less likely to plagiarize yourself if you move into a new field or a new style.

One problem is what is often called a lack of motivation. Aging scholars lose interest; they find it hard to get to work; they work slowly. It is easy to attribute this to a change in *them*, but we should not overlook a change in their world. For *motivation* read *reinforcement*. In old age, behavior is not as strongly reinforced. Biological aging weakens reinforcing consequences. Behavior is more and more likely to be followed by aches and pains and quick fatigue. Things tend to become "not worth doing" in the sense that the aversive consequences exact too high a price. Positive reinforcers become less common and less powerful. Poor vision closes off the world of art, faulty hearing the enjoyment of highly fidelitous music. Foods do not taste as good, and erogenous tissues grow less sensitive. Social reinforcers are attenuated. Interests and tastes are shared with a smaller number of people.

In a world in which our behavior is not generously reinforced we are said to lack zest, joie de vivre, interest, ambition, aspirations, and a hundred other desirable "states of mind" and "feelings." These are really the by-products of changed contingencies of reinforcement. When the occasion for strong behavior is lacking or when reinforcing consequences no longer follow, we are bored, discouraged, and depressed. But it is a mistake to say that we suffer from feelings. We suffer from the defective contingencies of reinforcement responsible for the feelings. Our environment is no longer maintaining strong behavior.

Our culture does not generously reinforce the behavior of old people. Both affluence and welfare destroy reinforcing contingencies, and so does retirement. Old people are not particularly important to younger people. Cicero made the point in his *De Senectute*: "Old age is honored only on condition that it defends itself, maintains its rights, is subservient to no one, and to its last breath rules over its own domain." We neglect that sage advice when we turn things over to another generation; we lose our position in the world and destroy important social reinforcers. Parents who turn their fortunes over to their children and then complain of neglect are the classical example, but aging scholars often do something of the same when they bring their work to an end expecting that they will be satisfied with well-deserved kudos. They find themselves out of date as the world moves forward.

A common reinforcer affects old age in a different though equally destructive way. Aging scholars come into possession of a unique stock-in-trade—their memories. They learn that they can hold a restless audience with personal reminiscences. "Thorndike? Oh, I knew him well." I have been guilty of a bit of that name-dropping myself when other reinforcers were in short supply, and I have been wallowing in reminiscence lately in writing my autobiography. The trouble is that it takes you backward. You begin to live your life in the wrong direction.

There are other things than memories to be exploited by the aged, and a careful assessment of one's possessions may be helpful. Harvey Lehman found that in certain fields—theoretical physics, for example—the best work was done well before the age of forty. What should theoretical physicists do with the rest of their lives? I once asked Lehman that question about myself (I trust that my personal reference to

Lehman has gripped you). I felt that my science was fairly rigorous, and perhaps I was near the end of a productive life as an experimentalist. What should I do with myself? "Administration," Lehman said. But I had been a department chairman, and that was not an attractive alternative. I turned instead to broader issues in the design of a culture, eventually publishing my conclusions in *Beyond Freedom and Dignity*.[1]

Something more than subject matter is involved. The whole repertoire we call intellectual is acquired when one is young. It survives as a lifestyle when one grows old, when it is much harder to execute. If intellectual behavior were as conspicuous as baseball, we would understand the problem. The solution may simply be to replace one repertoire with another. People who move from one city to another often suffer a brief depression, which appears to be merely the result of an old repertoire of behavior having become useless. The old stores, restaurants, theaters, and friends are no longer there. The depression is relieved by the acquisition of a new repertoire. It may be necessary in old age to acquire new ways of thinking, to adopt a new intellectual style, letting the size of the repertoire acquired in a long life offset the loss of skill in making use of it.

We should ask what we have written papers or books *for*. In the world of scholarship the answer is seldom money (if we exclude writers of potboiling textbooks), and in any case economic circumstances in old age are not easily improved. If the answer is commendation or fame, the problem may be extinction if commendation no longer follows, or satiation if there is a surfeit of commendation. Not much can be done about that, but a more likely explanation, and one that suggests helpful action, is that the scholar at his desk is not receiving the previously accustomed, immediate reinforcements: Sentences are not saying what they should say; solutions to problems remain out of reach; situations are not being effectively characterized; sequences are not in the right order; *sequiturs* are too often *non*.

Reinforcers need not occur too frequently if we are fortunate enough to have been reinforced on a good schedule. A

---

[1] B. F. Skinner, *Beyond freedom and dignity* (New York: Knopf, 1971).

"stretched variable-ratio schedule" refers to a process you have all experienced as you acquired a taste for good literature, a process in which the reinforcing moments occur much less often than in cheap literature. In a comic strip you laugh at the end of every four frames, and in cheap literature something interesting happens on almost every page. Learning to enjoy good literature is essentially learning to read for longer and longer periods of time before coming upon a moving passage—a passage all the more moving for having required a long preparation. Gambling is reinforced on a variable-ratio schedule, and pathological gamblers show the effect of a history in which they began with reasonable success and only later exhausted their resources. Many of the reinforcers in old age tend to be on a stretched variable-ratio schedule. The Marquis de Sade described many interesting examples. The same process may explain the persistence of the aging scholar. If your achievements as a thinker have been spaced on a favorable schedule, you will have no difficulty in remaining active even though current achievements are spaced far apart. Like the hooked gambler, you will enjoy your life as a thinker in spite of the negative utility.

An audience is a neglected, independent variable. What one says is determined in a very important way by the person one is talking to. But the retired teacher no longer talks with students, and the retired scientist no longer discusses work with colleagues. Old scholars find themselves spending time with people who are not interested in their field. They may receive fewer invitations to speak or find it harder to accept them. Those who will read the papers or books they are writing are much too far removed in time to serve as an audience. An appropriate measure of intellectual self-management is to organize discussions, if only in groups of two. Find someone with similar interests. Two heads together are better than both apart. In talking with another person we have ideas that do not occur when we are alone at our desk. Some of what we say may be borrowed from what the other says, but the mere effect of having someone to say it to is usually conspicuous.

In searching for an audience, beware of those who are trying to be helpful and too readily flatter you. Second childishness brings you back within range of those kindergarten teachers who exclaim, "But *that* is very *good!*" except that instead of saying, "My, you are really growing up!" they will say, "You are not really getting old!" As I have pointed out in Chapter 2, those who thoughtlessly help those who can help themselves work a sinister kind of destruction by making the good things in life no longer properly contingent on behavior. If you have been very successful, the most sententious stupidities will be received as pearls of wisdom, and your standards will instantly fall. If you are still struggling to be successful, flattery will more often than not put you on the wrong track by reinforcing useless behavior.

Well, there you have it. I have been batting that Ping-Pong ball back and forth long enough. I have reported some of the ways in which I have tried to avoid growing old as a thinker, and in addition I have given you a sample of the result. You may wish to turn to another comparison with a different species and conclude, if I may so paraphrase Dr. Johnson, "Sir, an aged lecturer is like a dog walking on his hinder legs. It is not done well; but you are surprised to find it done at all."

chapter 11

Can the Experimental Analysis of Behavior Rescue Psychology?

ટ•ટ•ટ•ટ•ટ•ટ•ટ•

In 1982 Nicholas Wade published an editorial note in *The New York Times* that read in part as follows:

> In the May issue of *Psychology Today*, 11 of "the best minds in the field" describe what each considers to be "the most significant work in psychology over the last decade and a half." The results are astonishing: it would seem that there has been none.
>
> "Significant work" implies work generally agreed to be important, but the 11 Best Minds in psychology agree on hardly anything. Stanley Milgram of the City University of New York hails the teaching of sign language to apes as an enduring recent achievement. But another contributor, Ulric Neisser of Cornell, cites as important the evident *failure* to teach sign language to apes.
>
> B. F. Skinner, alleging himself not well informed of recent progress in other fields of psychology, recounts the advances in behavioral psychology, which he pioneered. But two other sages, Jerome Bruner of the New School for Social Research and Richard Lazarus of Berkeley, laud the escape from Skinnerian psychology as the major achievement of the period. . . .
>
> Almost the only recent achievement hailed by more than one contributor is the discovery of endorphins, the brain's natural

painkillers. This is certainly an interesting development, but the credit belongs to pharmacologists and physiologists; psychology had little to do with it.

The failure of the 11 psychologists to agree on almost anything evinces a serious problem in their academic discipline. Physicists or biologists asked the same question would not concur on everything but there would be a substantial commonality in their answers. Can psychology be taken seriously as science if even its leading practitioners cannot agree on recent advances?[1]

That is a strong indictment of an established science in a prestigious newspaper. Unfortunately, many of us who call ourselves psychologists will agree with much of it. Psychology as a science is, in fact, in a shambles. Unwittingly, two of the contributors to that issue of *Psychology Today* have, I think, explained why. As Jerome Bruner puts it, there has been a "continued movement . . . away from the restrictive shackles of behaviorism."

Those who so triumphantly announce the death of behaviorism are announcing their own escape from the canons of scientific method. Psychology is apparently abandoning all efforts to stay within the dimensional system of natural science. It can no longer define its terms by pointing to referents, much less referents measurable in centimeters, grams, and seconds. It has returned to a hypothetical inner world. Bruner boasts of having rejoined the philosophers in the study of mind, language, values, and perception. Rollo May is pleased that "psychology has moved into matters that used to be left to poetry," and Philip Zimbardo suggests that cognitive science may now consider implanting a little soul.

There is no doubt of the freedom thus enjoyed. A great many things can be talked about when standards are less rigorous. The field of psychology has expanded enormously. The very divisions of the American Psychological Association suggest the current range—childhood development, personality, social issues, arts, clinical and other counseling, industry, education, public service, the military, aging, rehabilitation, philosophy, community, humanism, mental

---

[1]Nicholas Wade, "Smart apes, or dumb?" *New York Times*, April 30, 1982. Copyright © 1982 by The New York Times Company. Reprinted by permission.

retardation, ecology, family services, health, psychoanalysis, law, and so on. And a new feature of *The American Psychologist* is devoted to public policy. Unfortunately, as psychology has expanded in this way it has moved farther and farther from anything that could be called science.

One can admire the concern and compassion that lead people to consider these matters, and one can acknowledge the practical usefulness of much of what they say. One can admit that at the present time it is not always easy to say more in a scientific way; that has been true of all the sciences, especially in their early stages. There is still a part of human behavior with respect to which one must simply do one's best with the available resources. But if we are ever to do better, if concern and compassion are ever to be matched by achievement, it will be with a science of human behavior, and psychology once considered itself that science.

Part of what was called psychology has been lost to other fields. As the *Times* noted, the discovery of endorphins may be an advance, but it can scarcely be attributed to psychology, and physiology has taken over much more of the old territory. A field that once bestowed respectability on psychology—the study of sense organs in the name of the elements of consciousness—is now part of physiology and is studied with the instruments and methods of biological science. Psychologists such as Lashley, Hebb, and Klüver studied the brain, using a mixture of psychological and physiological methods, but neurology and biochemistry have taken over that field. In short, certain parts of the human organism are now being studied, as they should be, with the methods and concepts of physical and biological science.

That does not mean that cognitive psychologists have abandoned the brain. A touch of physiology is attractive because it seems to save them from dualism, and many of them use *brain* and *mind* interchangeably. Freud took a similar position much earlier. He assumed that we would some day know what the ego, superego, and id, the conscious, preconscious, and unconscious, and all the dynamisms *really were* in neurological terms. Chomsky has denied any ontological import in his references to mind (in other words, he does not claim to know the nature of the stuff of which it is

made). Rather, he is concerned with an "abstract charac-
terization of the properties of certain physical mechanisms."[2]
(His comment that they are "almost entirely unknown" will
be challenged by many physiologists.) In that issue of *Psychology Today* the cognitive psychologists are less hesitant
about ontology. Bruner, for example, tells us that the mind is
here to stay, presumably never to be replaced by a neurological account.

When statements about mind are offered as statements
about a model of what will eventually be described in physical
terms, we must ask whether it is the right model. There is
good reason to believe that it is not. The most popular is based
on the computer, which spurred the revival of cognitive science. The human organism, like a computer, is said to store
copies of the external world (as "representations") and to process them according to rules that are either part of a genetic
endowment or learned from experience. As I have pointed out
elsewhere,[3] representations and rules may be nothing more
than fanciful internalizations of contingencies of reinforcement. Behavior occurs in a given setting; the organism is
thereby changed and will behave differently in a similar setting later on. There is no evidence whatsoever that it stores a
copy of the setting or of the contingent relations among setting, behavior, and consequence. The external world remains
where it has always been—outside the organism. Rules
describe contingencies; they are not to be found *in* them or in
the organism that they have changed.

In following the Pied Piper of cognitive science, psychology has lost its hold upon reality. It is therefore more than
ever subject to the whims of fashion, to revisions and recon-
siderations, and to controversy. It is not surprising that it has
made so little progress. For more than a quarter of a century
we have been promised a new discipline that would tell us
what we have always wanted to know about knowledge and
thought. The promise has, I believe, not been kept. The free-

---

[2]N. Chomsky, *Rules and representations* (New York: Columbia University Press, 1980).
[3]See Chapter 7.

dom—the license—that cognitive science enjoys has been costly.

The experimental analysis of behavior, in contrast, is steadily building upon its past and proceeding in a reasonably ordered way to embrace more and more of what people are actually doing in the world at large. But has it also serious flaws? Certainly there have been rumblings. The Brelands' paper "The Misbehavior of Organisms" was an early example.[4] Herrnstein's "The Evolution of Behaviorism" was another.[5] And what about the Garcia Effect? Or autoshaping? And cannot all learned behavior be brought under the rubric of associationism? Let us look more closely at some of these apparent flaws.

The Breland Effect. A good example of the failure to understand the interaction of natural selection and operant conditioning is the use that has been made of the interesting facts reported by the Brelands in 1961. When Keller Breland first told the Harvard "Pigeon Staff" about them in 1960, we were impressed. Contrary to certain claims, we were far from "disturbed." Apparently an organism that has repeatedly manipulated an object as a token will sometimes begin to treat it like an object found in its natural habitat. There is no reason why, upon occasion, phylogenic behavior should not intrude in this way upon ontogenic behavior. Certainly intrusions in the other direction are common enough. Civilization shows the extent to which operant conditioning has suppressed phylogenic tendencies.

Superstition. The effect of an accidentally contingent reinforcer offers some of the best evidence of the power of operant conditioning, and possibly for that reason it has been challenged—as, for example, by Staddon and Simmelhag.[6] The behavior is said to drift toward phylogenic forms. I am

[4]K. Breland and M. Breland, *The American Psychologist,* 16 (1961), 681.

[5]R. J. Herrnstein, *The American Psychologist,* (1977).

[6]J. E. R. Staddon and V. L. Simmelhag, "The 'superstition' experiment: A reexamination of its implications for the principles of adaptive behavior," *Psychological Review,* 73, no. 1 (1971).

quite sure of my original observation.[7] I have repeated it many times, often as a surefire lecture demonstration. Deliver food every twenty seconds to a hungry pigeon and it will soon exhibit a food-getting ritual of unpredictable topography. I see no reason why there should not be a drift toward phylogenic behavior. It would be something like the Breland Effect unopposed by operant contingencies.

"Misleading" simplifications. In all the experimental sciences there is a fundamental practice: when studying one process, eliminate all others that may affect the data. Chemists use pure substances for obvious reasons. Physicists hold irrelevant variables constant. The experimental space used in analyzing behavior is as free as possible of distracting influences, including the releasers of innate behavior. Barry Schwartz has drawn a strange conclusion from this. Operant conditioners, he says, "capture the behavior of pigeons and rats in laboratory environments by eliminating possible biological influences." He goes on:

> The experimental chamber generally seems to prevent the occurrence of behaviors like these; hence the claim that it reveals universal principles. One must wonder, however, about whether any situation which prevents the occurrence of behaviors as powerful as these is not fundamentally distorting our understanding of the principles of behavior. It seems that if the conditioning chamber in fact prevents these sorts of species-typical behavior patterns, it cannot be telling us anything very important about the control of behavior in the natural environment.[8]

If that is true, ethologists are equally guilty when, in studying natural behavior in the field, they make sure that there has been no chance for conditioning. Must we conclude that they cannot therefore be telling us anything important about behavior in the natural environment?

Sociobiology. Ethology has spawned a child that threatens to play Oedipus and kill its father. It has also been

---

[7]B. F. Skinner, "'Superstition' in the pigeon," *Journal of Experimental Psychology*, 38 (1948), 168–72.

[8]B. Schwartz, "In pursuit of B. F. Skinner," *Swarthmore College Bulletin*, March 1981.

said to threaten the experimental analysis of behavior. The term, with its roots *bio-* and *socio-*, alludes to the roles played by genes in biology and society and thus skips over the individual. As I point out in Chapter 4, selection is a causal mode that is found only in living things. It operates at three levels. Darwin revealed its role in natural selection, but Herbert Spencer had already pointed out, if none too clearly, its role in the behavior of the individual and in the evolution of cultural practices.

A 1982 issue of *Science* contains an interview with Ernst Mayr,[9] a leading figure in evolutionary theory and the author of a book called *The Growth of Biological Thought.*[10] In explaining why evolutionary theory is misunderstood by physicists, Mayr neglects an important point about selection. As to the differences between physical and living systems, he says, "There isn't a process in a living organism that isn't completely consistent with any physical theory. Living organisms, however, differ from inanimate matter by the degree of the complexity of their systems and by the possession of a genetic program." Complexity itself is not a difference in kind, nor was the "organization" which biologists, at an earlier date, used in defining an organism. The "genetic program" points, though not directly, to the real difference: Organisms differ from physical things because they show selection by consequences.

In *Sociobiology*, E. O Wilson points to certain features common to natural selection, operant conditioning, and the evolution of cultures, and attributes them all to genes.[11] Genes no doubt explain behavior resulting from natural selection, and they are also responsible for operant conditioning as a process, but once that process has evolved, a different kind of selection accounts for the behavior of the individual and the evolution of cultural practices.

Autoshaping.   I studied another process said to threaten an operant analysis in the late 1940s and tried to get a gradu-

---

[9]R. Lewin, "Biology is not postage stamp collecting," *Science*, 216 (1982), 718–20.
[10]E. Mayr (Cambridge, Mass.: Harvard University Press, 1982).
[11]E. O. Wilson (Cambridge, Mass.: Harvard University Press, Belknap Press, 1975).

ate student to take it up for her thesis in 1950. In my experiment, a spot of light moved across a screen and when it reached one edge, a food magazine operated. A hungry pigeon began to peck the spot as if it were driving it across the screen. Epstein and I confirmed this result,[12] although it is not clear that the pigeon is driving the spot; it may be merely following it. In the mid 1950s, W. H. Morse and I were curious about the great variability in extinction following continuous reinforcement. After a given number of reinforcements, some pigeons would emit many hundreds of responses but others only a few. We thought the difference might be due to the fact that some pigeons often missed the key or pecked too lightly to operate it, in which case their pecking was therefore actually reinforced on an intermittent schedule. We made a very sensitive key and evoked a clear-cut exploratory response, using the method Brown and Jenkins later called *autoshaping*.[13] We spoke of it as "conditioning a hot key." (Incidentally, we got our answer, though we never published it. If you make sure that all responses are reinforced, you can reinforce many thousands of times and still get extinction in fewer than a hundred responses.) Organisms presumably possess a repertoire of innate behavior with which they explore unusual features of the environment. Through a kind of Pavlovian conditioning, a key that lights up before food is delivered becomes the kind of feature eliciting or releasing such a response. An article in the *Journal of the Experimental Analysis of Behavior* argues that some instances of Pavlov's "orienting reflex" may be examples.[14] That the response to the key may actually reduce the frequency of reinforcement should occasion no surprise.

Comments by two reviewers of *Autoshaping and Conditioning Theory* by Locurto, Terrace and Gibbon are relevant.[15] In *Contemporary Psychology* Barry Schwartz writes:

---

[12]R. Epstein and B. F. Skinner, "Resurgence of responding after the cessation of response-independent reinforcement," *Proceedings of the National Academy of Sciences*, 77, no. 10 (1980), 6251–53.

[13]P. L. Brown and H. M. Jenkins, "Autoshaping the pigeon's keypeck," *Journal of the Experimental Analysis of Behavior*, 11 (1968), 1–8.

[14]Gyorgy Buzsaki, "The 'Where is it?' reflex: Autoshaping the orienting response," *Journal of the Experimental Analysis of Behavior*, 37 (1982), 461–84.

[15]C. M. Locurto, H. S. Terrace, and J. Gibbon, *Autoshaping and conditioning theory*

The key is lit, and then food is delivered. Procedurally, this is a mundane example of classical conditioning, with the key as a CS and food as a US. But what is the classically conditioned response? It is not salivation, or an eye blink; it is a peck at the key. The classically conditioned response is, or seems to be, what used to be viewed as a voluntary response, not a reflex. What is going on? Is the key peck voluntary or reflexive? Is autoshaping classical or instrumental? Is there something wrong with our distinction between the two conditioning processes?[16]

There is nothing wrong except Schwartz's analysis. An operant cannot be identified by topography alone; the controlling variables must be specified. When several different variables are operative, as in verbal behavior, a structural or formalistic approach is especially troublesome, as linguists are learning to their sorrow. Pecking a key is an operant when it is due primarily to a particular history of reinforcement. It is a released innate response when the lighting of a key is followed by the presentation of food, as in the autoshaping procedure.

Schwartz draws another supposedly threatening conclusion:

What autoshaping suggested was that pecking might indeed be special—peculiar to pigeons (and perhaps other birds) in feeding situations. In consequence, it raised the serious possibility that the massive accumulation of empirical generalizations about the determinants of pigeons' pecking might not be applicable to all the instrumental behavior of all organisms. Instead, these generalizations might only be true of pigeons—or of organisms in situations in which the required instrumental response was biologically related to the reinforcer.

But pigeons can press levers and rats can peck keys and will do so under appropriate contingencies of reinforcement. As I pointed out in *The Behavior Analyst*, there are several kinds of pigeon pecks, and they are not all concerned with

(New York: Academic Press, 1981).

[16]B. Schwartz, "Autoshaping: Driving toward a psychology of learning," *Contemporary Psychology*, 26 (1981), 823–25.

ingestion.[17] Ferster and I explicitly acknowledged the ethological sources of the pecking response we studied.

In a review of the same book in *Science*, Peter Killeen says that "in 1968 Brown and Jenkins demonstrated that Pavlovian contingencies (pairing a key light with food in a standard experimental chamber) yielded faster conditioning of the pigeon's key pecks than did traditional hand-shaping procedures."[18] His next sentence begins, "As if this were not bad enough . . . ." How bad it is depends on who does the shaping. Pavlovian conditioning is certainly slower than operant conditioning: I know of no instance in which one pairing has been shown to be effective (Pavlov's record-breaking dog showed a small effect after five pairings of tone and food). But as I reported some fifty years ago, a single reinforcement of pressing a lever may be followed by a sizable extinction curve. I daresay the same thing can be shown for pecking a key. Killeen also says that the work on autoshaping means that the discipline is moving close to the biological bases of behavior, "a position it was a mistake ever to have left." I should like to know who has left it.

The Garcia Effect.   Many years ago taste aversion was known as "stomach memory." The unusual thing about it is the time that elapses between behavior and consequence. In operant conditioning, a reinforcing consequence must be closely contingent upon behavior. If it were not, all intervening behavior would also be reinforced and chaos would follow. Yet in the Garcia Effect a tendency to eat a particular food is affected by consequences occurring many hours later. The result has obvious survival value in protecting organisms from the further ingestion of poisons or highly indigestible foodstuffs. Presumably the punishing consequence would affect the eating of any other unusual foodstuff at the same time or during the interval, but not other kinds of behavior. There is little chance for confusion, because the effect is a

---

[17]B. F. Skinner, "The species-specific behavior of ethologists," *The Behavior Analyst*, 3 (1980), 51.

[18]P. Killeen, "A challenge to learning theory," *Science*, 214 (1981), 548.

special consequence of ingestion. If other kinds of deferred punitive consequences had a comparable effect, it would be felt by all intervening behavior. There is nothing in the Garcia Effect that contradicts any part of an operant analysis or throws into question any established fact. The consequence is punishing rather than positively reinforcing and seems to work exactly as I describe punishment in *Science and Human Behavior*. Through Pavlovian conditioning, stimuli arising from a situation in which behavior has been punished become aversive, and any behavior resulting in their reduction or removal is reinforced as escape or avoidance.

Probability of reinforcement. In an operant chamber the organism is in contact with the contingencies only at the moment of reinforcement. Ferster and I designed much of our research to show that schedules have their appropriate effects by virtue of the stimuli present at just that time—stimuli generated in part by the organism's recent behavior. Several writers have recently implied that organisms may be sensitive to an increase in the mere probability of reinforcement when no reinforcer is immediately contingent upon a response. I do not think that the possibility of a conditioned reinforcer has been satisfactorily eliminated as an explanation, but I will rest my case on the following experiment, which takes advantage of the fact that the role of a reinforcer is clearer in shaping behavior than in maintaining it. Let small measures of food be delivered to a hungry pigeon at two different rates—once a minute and three times a minute, for example, not equally spaced. The experimenter holds a switch with which the rate can be changed from the low to the high rates, and is asked to use it to shape a bit of behavior—say, a clockwise turn. Superstitious responses will emerge, and it is conceivable that one of them will be turning, but that will happen only if there is an accidentally contingent reinforcement. If the rates are very fast—say, ten times a minute and thirty times a minute—the repeated delivery of food may serve as a conditioned stimulus and accidental contingencies will be much more likely. But at the rates of delivery that are said to show an effect on the maintenance of behavior, I predict that no effect will be demonstrated.

"Learning processes." Another source of misunderstanding of the relation between operant conditioning and natural selection is the strong inclination to look inside a system to see what makes it tick. Those who use operant conditioning are criticized when they refuse to do so. They are said to be interested in controlling behavior but not in understanding the mechanisms responsible for it. I am sure there are mechanisms, but they belong to a different discipline—physiology. Whether there are two processes of conditioning or only one is not a question about behavior, because the external contingencies in respondent and operant conditioning are clearly different. Both may occur in the same setting, but even so they can be easily distinguished. The question is about a common process—an inferred mechanism.

The inferred mechanism is usually discussed as associationism. Pavlov's dog is said to have associated the bell and the food, but as I have pointed out, it was Pavlov who associated them, that is, who put them together side by side.[19] There is no evidence that the dog engages in any such process internally. Incidentally, I am not sure that Pavlovian conditioning is a good model of associationism. Though I have used the expression, I now think that the term *stimulus substitution* is misleading. Too often there is no unconditioned stimulus. In the Estes-Skinner experiment, for example, a tone that is repeatedly followed by shock soon suppresses any operant behavior in progress, but a shock alone does not suppress the behavior. In autoshaping, similarly, the response to the key need not be the type of response elicited by the reinforcer. Jenkins and Moore have shown a slight similarity of the autoshaping peck to the consummatory responses of eating and drinking, but they note that exceptions have been reported by others. Autoshaping is not a "mundane example of classical conditioning." The salivary response has idiosyncratic properties that are rare, even in other autonomic responses. Reflex responses or released behaviors have evolved that have no unconditioned stimuli or releasers. Stimuli must acquire the power to elicit or release such behavior during the lifetime of the individual. They acquire

---

[19]B. F. Skinner, "Why I am not a cognitive psychologist," *Behaviorism*, 5 (1977), 1–10.

this power when they precede positive reinforcers (as in auto-shaping) or negative reinforcers (as in the Estes-Skinner effect). Some examples of association, particularly those involving emotional responses, may show a substitution of stimuli as in Pavlov's experiments, but many are clearly operant and have to do with the pairing of discriminative stimuli.

As long as we study observed behavior as a function of genetic and environmental variables, we are on safe ground. We shall no doubt continue to discover new facts, some of which may be puzzling but, if we are to judge from the past, will eventually be assimilated by that corpus of knowledge at the heart of the experimental analysis of behavior. But how will historians of science treat the digressions I have just examined? I hope they will see that the critics of an experimental analysis of behavior have not properly understood it. Recently I was heartened when a psychiatrist sent me a book he had just published, containing the following passage:

> E. L. Thorndike, as early as 1890, demonstrated in a very convincing way the ability of animals to learn if a reward is given them. In the "Skinner box," a test animal put into a closed box will vainly search for an escape hole. A lever connected to an invisible opening, if touched accidentally, will permit escape. As the experiment is repeated several times, the animal—rat, mouse, hamster, monkey or otherwise—will take less and less time to find the solution of escape by touching the lever. Ultimately the animal becomes most proficient.

A passage like that is consoling because it makes one realize how far some of the critics of an operant analysis are from understanding it.

So-called objections to operant theory need not detain us. There is work to be done. My own contribution to that issue of *Psychology Today* read in part as follows:

> I am inclined to rank progress in basic laboratory analysis first. With the aid of miniaturized controlling equipment and computers, behavior is now observed and measured with increasing precision in operant laboratories throughout the world. Repertoires of behavior are being studied which have a much greater breadth and complexity. It is still a hallmark of the operant-conditioning method . . . that the results may be

formulated in centimeters, grams, and seconds rather than in the nonphysical dimensions of mental life.

These advances have greatly increased the extent to which the terms and principles drawn from an experimental analysis can be used in interpreting behavior in the world at large. Interpretation has not been well analyzed by scientific methodologists, and it has been widely misunderstood by critics of the operant field. Among the processes which have been submitted to more careful analysis and interpretation are many that have been attributed to . . . concept formation, creativity, and decision-making. A number of these are being clarified as an operant analysis, particularly of verbal behavior, is better understood. Some behavior is contingency-shaped; it has been selected by reinforcing consequences in the past. [Other behavior may consist of] imitating the behavior of, or following the advice of, another person whose behavior has already been selected by its consequences. This distinction between rule-directed and contingency-shaped behavior is only one example of a new approach to the analysis of so-called cognitive processes.

One advantage in relating behavior directly to environmental conditions is that one can then move directly to technological control. An experimental analysis points to the conditions which must be changed to bring about changes in behavior for practical purposes.

Interest in the experimental analysis of behavior and its use in interpretation and practical control has spread rapidly throughout the world during the last 15 years. Associations have been organized and annual conferences held in the United States, Latin America, Europe, Israel, Japan, and elsewhere. The Association for Behavior Analysis, an international organization, attracts new members each year and its programs show an increasing scope.

Philosophers, political scientists, economists, and others who once dismissed behaviorism as rat psychology are now seriously considering its implications. The journal *Behaviorism*, with its large international board of editors, now in its 10th year, has become an important forum.

I myself am most concerned with the possible relevance of a behavioral analysis to the problems of the world today . . . . If there are solutions to those problems. I believe that they will be found in the kind of understanding to which an experimental analysis of human behavior points.

The experimental analysis of behavior is alive and well. Psychology needs it.

chapter 12

The Contrived
Reinforcer

ર્શા ર્શા ર્શા ર્શા ર્શા ર્શા

There is nothing new about the modification of behavior. Teachers have always modified the behavior of their students and students the behavior of their teachers. Employers have always modified the behavior of employees and employees the behavior or their employers. Therapists modify the behavior of those they help and those who are helped the behavior of their therapists. Governors modify the behavior of the governed and the governed the behavior of governors. Parents modify the behavior of their children and children the behavior of their parents. As friends, lovers, and acquaintances we modify the behavior of each other. The only thing that is new is the better understanding of how we do so derived from an experimental analysis of behavior. Those who claim to be changing minds or feelings through persuasion or argument are really changing behavior by changing its consequences. Through behavior modification we are said to *intervene* in the lives of others and *manipulate* them, and whether we should do so is an ethical question, but it is a question that can be answered by looking at other consequences.

Sugar is a strong reinforcer for the human species. We put sugar on some of the foods we eat because our behavior in doing so is reinforced by the consequence. At one time a susceptibility to reinforcement by sugar had great survival value because there were only a few sweet foods and they were often especially nutritious. A high susceptibility to reinforcement by sugar promoted extremely valuable behavior. Whether we should eat sugar now is a question about another consequence. In the world today the susceptibility leads to obesity and illness.

We put sugar on the food we give children because they are then more likely to eat it. If our behavior in doing so has been reinforced by the fact that their health is improved, we shall be commended, but not if the important consequence is getting breakfast out of the way without trouble. When manufacturers coat breakfast cereals with sugar and claim that they do so because children then eat a better breakfast, we look for still another consequence.

The systematic use of operant conditioning "for a purpose"—that is, because the use has reinforcing consequences for the user—has been widely debated. Sometimes the complaint is that consequences are not natural. In *The Shaping of a Behaviorist* I reported a bit of behavior modification in our daughter Deborah when she was about nine months old.[1] I was holding her on my lap, and when the room grew dark, I turned on a table lamp beside the chair. She smiled brightly, and I decided to test the light as a reinforcer. I turned it off, waited until she lifted her left hand slightly, and then turned it on and off quickly. Almost immediately she lifted her hand again, and again I turned the light on and off. I waited for bigger movements, and she was soon raising her arm in a wide arc "to turn on the light."

Because I had contrived those contingencies, I could be said to have *manipulated* her behavior. But suppose I had simply put a rattle in her hand and she had moved it, heard it rattle, and shaken it vigorously. Would it be said that I—or,

---

[1]B. F. Skinner, *The shaping of a behaviorist* (New York: Knopf, 1979), 293.

for that matter, nature—had been guilty of manipulation? In both cases the simple fact was that a movement of the arm was followed by a reinforcing event, but there were other consequences. Although we do not give babies rattles *in order to* make them wave their arms, the babies are happier and less likely to fret. Only if Deborah had accidentally come upon something that rattled and had begun to shake it vigorously would there be no charge of intervention or manipulation. In that case the consequence responsible for her behavior would be found in the survival value of such an effect on the evolution of the species.

Natural consequences can, in fact, be troublesome. Certain inadequacies in the evolution of operant conditioning lead, for example, to superstitious behavior, which is usually wasteful if not harmful. There are many natural systems that stretch a mean variable-ratio schedule to the point at which, as in the case of the pathological gambler, the behavior is called irrational. Sugar is only one of the reinforcers to which a susceptibility evolved in a very different environment and is now out of date. Indeed, it could be argued that the human species has reached its present position largely because cultures have managed to shield the individual from the reinforcing effects of the natural environment.

Nevertheless, natural reinforcing contingencies have much to be said for them. They are usually much more effectively contingent upon the topography of the behavior (the noise of the rattle was more precisely contingent upon movement than the flashes of light) and the occasion upon which it occurs (shaking the rattle was more likely to be evoked on similar occasions than raising the arm). In general, by allowing natural contingencies to take control whenever possible we generate behavior that is more likely to be appropriate to any occasion upon which it may occur again, and in doing so we promote the survival of the individual, the culture, and the species.

Education offers good examples. The earliest consequences in education, not to be confused with the education that occurs in daily life, were contrived: schoolboys (there were no schoolgirls) were beaten when they did not study. The connection between studying and avoiding aversive stimulation was certainly not a natural one. Corporal punishment has now been largely replaced by other aversive consequences, but it is still true that most students study to avoid the consequences of not studying. A long line of educators, beginning with Rousseau and ending, perhaps, with John Dewey and his followers, tried to replace these contrived consequences with natural ones. They also sought to replace aversive consequences with positively reinforcing ones. It was a plausible move: Children learn in real life without the help of contrived aversive contingencies; why should they not do so when being taught? It was only necessary to bring real life into the classroom or make the real world an educational environment. A child should learn to read or write only when the natural consequences were important.

It has taken several decades to discover that there are no natural consequences that can be efficiently used to shape the early stages of reading and writing. The behavior is too much the product of an advanced culture. Special contingencies must be contrived. (Only later will reading and writing have uncontrived consequences.) A number of learning centers in the United States provide a good example. Following instructions from cassette recorders, students respond on work sheets and their behavior is immediately reported as correct or incorrect by a magic-ink effect. There is no natural connection between responding correctly to a word or passage and the appearance of a particular mark on a paper, but under these conditions children learn to read quickly and easily. It is only later that the reinforcers that writers put into their work come into play.

It is a lesson we might have learned from the rattle. Why is the production of a light or noise reinforcing? We can understand why nature should have given nutritious food reinforcing properties—or, to put it correctly, why a susceptibility to reinforcement by certain properties of nutritious foods should have had survival value and hence should have been selected as a characteristic of the species—but what is the survival value of making a noise? A similar question has been asked about the survival value of play. The fighting play of young puppies is no doubt a stage in their maturation, but it is also a stage in which rudimentary forms of behavior are modified and made more effective by their consequences. Consequences having no survival value in themselves shape behavior that will be more effective when the consequences begin to contribute to survival. Play is a kind of education for life. As nature prepares the puppy to be a serious fighter by contriving consequences that shape effective play, so the educator contrives contingencies that make it possible for the student to act effectively in uncontrived circumstances later on. Much the same thing may be said for many aspects of therapy. By contriving relatively unambiguous social contingencies, the therapist builds a repertoire that will be naturally effective in the client's daily life.

The contrived contingencies of both education and therapy must eventually be terminated. Teacher or therapist must withdraw from the life of student or client before teaching or therapy can be said to be complete. Rousseau stated a preference for natural reinforcement with a useful phrase: the student must become "dependent on things," where "things" include people who are not acting as teachers or therapists.

There are two fields, however, in which it is usually believed that contrived contingencies must be maintained indefinitely. One is economics. The first "production of goods" must have had natural consequences. Food was immediately contingent on gathering and, later, on harvesting after planting and cultivating. A useful club or a digging stick was contingent upon fashioning it. Contrived economic reinforcers arose with the exchange of goods—when, for example, a person gathered food and exchanged it for a digging stick. The gathering was reinforced by the stick, which was not naturally connected with the behavior. Since barter necessarily involves two or more people, it is largely a system of contrived consequences, and money is, of course, the archetypal contrived reinforcer.

Modern industry is all too aware of its faults. Contrived reinforcers are seldom sharply contingent on the topography of the behavior. Artisans are more likely to work industriously and skillfully because certain features of what they make are naturally contingent upon the making, whereas the wages paid for production-line work are much less closely related to what the worker does. A supervisor with the power to discharge is needed to offset this weakness. Pay by the day or week is often mistakenly called reinforcement; its real function is to establish a standard of living from which the worker can be cut off. An authority recently said that production in industry "depends in great part on subordination, discipline, and acceptance of managerial authority." Note that no reference is made to any positively reinforcing consequences, natural or contrived.

The contrived reinforcer called money remains effective only when it has been exchanged for strongly reinforcing goods. In the nineteenth century the problem was solved with a hungry labor force, but today the goods for which wages are exchanged are much less essential. Social security and health insurance have changed the conditions under which money is reinforcing. Industrial managers therefore look for other reinforcers—the good opinion of the worker's associates, a closer contact with the product, and so on, and these are much more likely to be natural consequences.

A second field in which it is generally believed that contrived reinforcement must be maintained is government. The consequences are frankly aversive. The first contingencies were probably natural: People behaved well because of the reactions of those whom they affected. We still often obey people with superior power because by doing so we terminate the conditioned aversive stimulus called a "threat of punishment." The consequence is closely contingent upon the topography of the behavior, but when the power to punish is assigned to a government, the contingencies are more likely to be contrived and their shortcomings evident. Courts of law are needed to decide when a law has been violated and when punitive consequences are therefore to be imposed. The consequences are not only less clearly contingent upon the topography of the behavior, they are delayed. Governmental practices tend to move farther and farther from natural, face-to-face contingencies. We can restore some of the advantages in that control by returning to small groups, such as intentional communities. There are few if any contrived reinforcers in Walden Two, for example. The community has been designed in such a way that it naturally reinforces the behavior needed to maintain it, without the mediation of a government or industrial organization. Unfortunately, it is not easy to see how the world as a whole can dispense with governments and economic systems in that way.

Another anecdote about my daughter bears on a different use of contrived contingencies. When she was three or four years old I was talking with her at bedtime and rubbing her back. I decided to test rubbing as a reinforcer. I waited until she lifted her foot slightly and then rubbed briefly. Almost immediately she lifted her foot again, and again I rubbed. Then she laughed. "What are you laughing at?" I said. "Every time I raise my foot you rub my back!" She had quite precisely described the contingencies I had contrived.

Cognitive psychologists would say that she had discovered and stated a rule. They would also say that even when she was nine months old she must have discovered the rule that she should raise her arm to turn on the light. Children are said to discover the rules of grammar when they learn to talk. That is one of the mistakes that arise from the concept of knowledge or cognition. A hungry rat presses a lever, receives food, and is then more likely to press again when hungry. That is what we observe. But cognitive psychologists say that the rat has learned, and now *knows*, that pressing the lever brings food. A description of the contingencies has somehow been moved into the head of the rat in the form of information or knowledge.

That contention seems more plausible with a human subject because we can apparently impart the same knowledge in a different way—simply by saying, "If you press the lever, you will get food." In other words we can describe the contingencies rather than use them to shape behavior. I could not have told the nine-month-old Deborah to lift her arm because she had not yet learned to respond to that kind of verbal stimulus, but three years later I could have told her to lift her foot. Why should I have bothered to shape the behavior? Why not dispense with contingencies altogether, whether natural or contrived, and impart knowledge in a more efficient way?

The answer concerns a problem cognitive psychologists have not solved. Contingencies of reinforcement are said to both inform and motivate, but the concept of knowledge refers only to information. Motivation must be treated separately. We can state a rule, but we must also make sure that it will be followed, and in doing so we find ourselves back again with contingencies of reinforcement.

Contingencies are needed first of all to teach people to follow rules. People must become effective listeners, and that means they must acquire all the behavior that can be specified in rules if they are to do what the rules describe. Much more important are the contingencies under which they will continue to follow the rules once they have learned them. Early examples of "rule-governed behavior" were presumably the responses people made to orders or commands. A command specifies behavior to be executed and at least implies the (usually) aversive consequences of not executing it. The rules of religious organizations are codifications of orders or commands; they identify potentially punishable behavior and identify or imply the (usually) punitive consequences of disobedience. The laws of governments are more explicit.

Because the word *rule* retains something of the coercive nature of contrived aversive contingencies, it does not well describe statements of contingencies involving happier consequences. Advice is an example. To a friend arriving in a new city you say, "If you like good Italian food, go to Luigi's." By following that advice, the friend can avoid sampling all the Italian restaurants in town. Taking the advice will have natural rather than contrived consequences, and as a result the friend will be more likely to take advice from you and other friends in the future. A warning ("Luigi's is expensive") refers to a different kind of consequence that is also not contrived by the adviser.

The word *rule* also does not well describe the verbal stimuli called directions and instructions. We follow instructions for assembling a piece of equipment if comparable behavior has had reinforcing consequences—namely, the possession of properly assembled equipment. We follow instructions in learning how to operate a new piece of equipment if similar instructions have led to effective behavior. We learn to drive a car when someone tells or shows us what to do. (Showing could be called *verbal* in the sense that it would have no effect if a viewer were not present.) Our behavior is at first entirely under the control of the instructions, but the behavior of the car on the road begins to supply natural consequences, and when we have eventually become skillful drivers, we forget the instructions.

Proverbs and maxims are generalized advice, accumulated and transmitted by cultures. The maxim "To lose a friend, lend him money" identifies behavior (lending) and a contingent consequence (loss of a friend). The consequences of observing the maxim are not contrived. The "laws" of science allude to natural consequences and are therefore closer to advice, maxims, and instructions than to the laws of religions and governments.

In general, rules are followed and advice taken only because of consequences experienced in similar arrangements in the past. When there is no relevant personal history, a contract is used. A contract describes contingent relations between behavior and consequence: "If you do this, I will do that." Additional aversive consequences of a failure to act are usually implied, if only the loss of the positive consequence specified. The trouble with contracts is that the behavior will not necessarily be more likely to occur again in the absence of a contract. Nevertheless, contracts may be useful as instruction if natural contingencies are waiting to take over.

There is no point in advising, instructing, or ordering a person to do something that cannot be done. "Don't worry" is seldom, if ever, effective advice, because the behavior is respondent rather than operant. Advice such as "Love your enemies" or "Show more affection to your unlovable child" may be hard to follow. Nevertheless, operant behavior associated with not worrying or loving or being affectionate may have reinforcing consequences. Some effect on the autonomic nervous system may even occur as a by-product.

Advice, rules, laws, and other descriptions of contingencies are important to a culture because they enable the individual to profit from the experience of those who have experienced common contingencies and described them in useful ways. But what about contingencies that have never been experienced by anyone? From statements about experienced contingencies, for example, logicians and mathematicians deduce statements about unexperienced contingencies that prove useful. New rules are derived from old. From statements about experienced instances, scientists infer general statements embracing new instances. We respond to these descriptions, as we take advice in general, only if responding under similar circumstances has had reinforcing consequences. The "authority" of logicians, mathematicians, and scientists, and the "trust" we place in them come from our experience in following the rules they derive. Our inclination to respond may also be stronger if a deduction or reference has been proved, in the sense of being derived in more than one way or confirmed in more than one instance. In general the contingencies involve natural consequences.

Advice involving consequences that have not been experienced but are predicted statistically is hard to take. You are warned that if you continue to smoke you will be much more likely to die of lung cancer or a heart attack, but the warning seldom if ever comes from one who has experienced the contingencies and is now dying. Nor are you likely to heed that warning because you have heeded an equally serious one with reinforcing results. If you stop smoking, it will not be because of the statistics but because someone has contrived other consequences. A government contrives other consequences by making it illegal to buy cigarettes (as it does in the case of minors), by suppressing advertising that portrays smoking as admirable and healthful (as it does on television), by making cigarettes more expensive through taxation, by withdrawing financial support from tobacco farmers, and (probably least effective) requiring that a warning be printed on each pack of cigarettes. Educators, therapists, and friends censure and complain and reinforce nonsmoking by withdrawing contrived aversive stimuli.

Contrived reinforcers are necessary when natural consequences are long deferred. How do we "take the distant future into account"? We can respond fairly well with respect to the immediate future for several reasons. The selective action of operant conditioning (like natural selection) prepares us for a future more or less resembling the past. We also respond to statements about the future made by those who have experienced a possibly similar past. The statistical predictions just mentioned are based on events that have already taken place, and we observe the laws of logic, mathematics, and science because of past consequences of doing so. But what about events that have no precedent—events that have never occurred in the experience of anyone?

Certain predictions about the future of the world are of this sort. Something may be happening for the first time. It can be predicted with some accuracy, but the future of the species may depend upon whether there can ever be any contingencies of reinforcement, contrived or natural, that will induce us to act upon those predictions. We may "know" that certain things are going to happen, but knowing is not enough; action is needed. Why should it occur? That is perhaps the most terrifying question in the history of the human species. It will be answered, if at all, by someone who knows a great deal about contrived reinforcement.

chapter 13

Pavlov's Influence
on Psychology
in America

ช่ะช่ะช่ะช่ะช่ะช่ะ

It is hard to think of oneself as a contemporary of a man who died nearly fifty years ago, but it is nonetheless true that on two occasions Pavlov and I worked on the same problem at the same time. I mention this for what it may be worth in supporting my right to comment on Pavlov's contribution to psychology. I am not an authority on Pavlov, and I shall report here little more than what I learned about his research as a student and then as it affected my own work and the work of those of whom I have remained a contemporary for a much longer period of time.

That American psychologists learned about Pavlov through German publications is clear from the fact that they first spelled his name with w's instead of v's. In 1909 R. M. Yerkes and S. Morgulis published "The Method of Pawlow in Animal Psychology."[1] Neither author seems to have been much influenced by Pavlov's work, but John B. Watson was, and fortunately I can let him tell his own story. In 1937

---

[1]Robert M. Yerkes and S. Morgulis, "The method of Pawlow in animal psychology," *Psychological Bulletin*, 6 (1909), 257–73.

Ernest R. Hilgard asked Watson the question, and he has kindly permitted me to give you Watson's answer:

> I cannot say that either Pavlov or Bechterev had much influence in shaping my early convictions. I never thought either of them was an objectivist. As a matter of fact, in a seminar I gave on Bechterev's Objective Psychology, I repeatedly pointed out that he was a parallelist at heart.
>
> I felt the same about Pavlov. Even in 1911 and 1912 when I was publishing my own views, neither had helped me much. I had worked the thing out in terms of HABIT formation. It was only later, when I began to dig into the vague word HABIT that I saw the enormous contribution Pavlov had made, and how easily the conditioned response could be looked upon as the unit of what we had all been calling HABIT. I certainly, from that point on, gave the master his due credit.
>
> Pavlov's work and the work of his students were so much more accurate and comprehensive in technique that it is small wonder he received the credit over Bechterev. Please don't get the impression that I discount Bechterev's work in any way. We used to correspond and I had made all arrangements for Lashley to go to him when the war broke out.
>
> Lashley deserves far more credit than I for the early conditioned reflex in this country. You will remember that I said he had done most of the work in my presidential address. [Watson's address was published as "The Place of the Conditioned Reflex in Psychology" in 1916.[2] In it he considered Pavlov's work on sensory discrimination as an alternative to introspection.]
>
> It has been a long time since I've read the old article of mine in the *Encyclopaedia Britannica* on Behaviorism. I think I wrote it about 1928. Possibly my memory was fresher then on those to whom credit is due.[3]

What Watson remembered in 1928 was this:

> The work of Pawlow and his students on the conditioned reflex, while known to the behaviourists, played at first a relatively minor role in their formulations. This was due to the fact that his experiments were chiefly concerned with conditioned glandular reflexes, which was at that time a subject hardly touched upon by psychologists. Bechterev's work on the conditioned

---

[2]John B. Watson, *Psychological Review*, 23 (1916), 89–117.
[3]John H. Watson, letter to Ernest R. Hilgard, 1937.

motor reflex, where human subjects were used, had from the first a very much greater influence upon behaviourism. The work of Lashley in conditioning the human salivary reflex and of Watson and Rayner on conditioning human emotional reaction (fear) showed the great range of application of the conditioned reflex methods to human behaviour. This work has led to an attempt to formulate all habit (organization) in terms of conditioned glandular and motor reaction. In spite of the fact that behaviourism did not at first utilize to any extent the conditioned reflex methods, Pawlow and Bechterev must be looked upon as furnishing the keystone to its arch. During the period of the general formulation of behaviourism as a system rather than as an approach to psychology, or as a specialized method in psychology, the writings of E. B. Holt, A. P. Weiss, and K. S. Lashley are noteworthy.[4]

As Watson said, a salivary response was not of great interest to American psychologists, and subsequent work on the responses of glands and smooth muscles was not extensive. Lashley invented a method of collecting saliva from the parotid gland in humans, but in his *Brain Mechanisms and Intelligence*, published in 1929, he refers only a few times to conditioning, and then critically.[5] In 1922 Hulsey Cason reported a conditioned pupillary reflex.[6] and some work was done on the galvanic skin response, but the best known psychologists in the 1920s were almost untouched. Walter S. Hunter made very little use of Pavlov's work, although in 1933 a student of his, C. V. Hudgins, published an account of an attempt to reduce voluntary behavior to a conditioned reflex. (A subject said "Contract" and a bright light was flashed in her eye. Eventually the pupil contracted when she said "Contract.") Edward C. Tolman rejected the conditioned reflex formula in its entirety. In 1929 Clark L. Hull wrote a paper called "A Functional Interpretation of the Conditioned Reflex."[7] Hull was responsible for much of the interest in Pavlov during the next decade. In 1932 one of his students, W.

---

[4]*Encyclopaedia Britannica*, 14th ed. S. V. "Behaviorism."

[5]Karl S. Lashley, *Brain mechanisms and intelligence* (Chicago: University of Chicago Press, 1929).

[6]Hulsey Cason, "The conditioned pupillary reaction," *Journal of Experimental Psychology*, 5 (1922), 108–46.

[7]Clark L. Hull, *Psychological Review*, 36 (1929), 498–511.

M. Lepley, suggested that the conditioned reflex might explain verbal learning, and for years Hull referred to this as the Lepley Hypothesis. However, in his *Principles of Behavior*, published in 1943, he does not mention Lepley.[8]

In the thirties, Hilgard and Marquis studied the conditioned eyelid reflex.[9] With its double innervation this reflex raised a new issue, which became clearest when Americans turned to the so-called conditioned motor reflexes of Bechterev. In 1924 Watson published a paper on conditioned finger withdrawal, and in 1930 one of Hull's students, Helen Wolfle, investigated certain temporal properties of that reflex.[10] In 1928 Harold Schlosberg reported a conditioned knee jerk,[11] and in the same year Howard Liddell published his extensive work on conditioned leg flexion in sheep.[12]

The trouble was that these arrangements involved consequences of behavior as well as antecedents. The organism escaped from or avoided an aversive stimulus—a puff of air in the case of the eyelid reflex or an electric shock in the case of finger withdrawal or leg flexion. The issue was not clarified for some time. In his article in the *Encylopaedia Britannica* Watson traced a concern with the consequences of behavior to C. Lloyd Morgan and Edward L. Thorndike. Much later Tolman spoke of "purposive behavior" and used mazes that seemed to show the goal-directedness of behavior. In 1928 two Polish physiologists, J. Konorski and S. Miller, added a consequence to a reflex. They delivered a shock to the leg of a dog, and after the leg flexed, they gave the dog food. Eventually the dog flexed its leg in the absence of the shock. In November 1931 Konorski and Miller went to Leningrad to persuade Pavlov to change his theory. In a meeting on 20 April 1932 (one of the meetings that came to be called Pavlov's Wednes-

---

[8]Clark L. Hull, *Principles of behavior* (New York: Appleton-Century, 1943).

[9]Ernest R. Hilgard, "Reinforcement and inhibition of eyelid reflexes," *Journal of General Psychology*, 8 (1933), 85–113.

[10]Helen M. Wolfle, "Time factors in conditioning finger-withdrawal," *Journal of General Psychology*, 4 (1930), 372–79.

[11]Harold A. Schlosberg, "A study of the conditioned patellar reflex," *Journal of Experimental Psychology*, 11 (1928), 468–94.

[12]Howard S. Liddell and O. D. Anderson, "Certain characteristics of formation of conditioned reflexes in sheep," *Proceedings of the Society of Experimental Biology and Medicine*, 26 (1928), 81–82.

days) Pavlov mentioned Konorski and Miller, and credited them with having made conditioned reflexes into "conditioned stimuli for either attractive or noxious substances."[13]

I was struggling with the same problem at that time. I had been impressed by Pavlov's *Conditioned Reflexes*,[14] and in my early publications I referred to the behavior I was studying (pressing a lever) as a reflex. But as I have pointed out in *The Shaping of a Behaviorist*,[15] before publishing my results I distinguished between two types of conditioning: "In Type I, as in Pavlov's experiment, a new reflex is formed. The dog salivates in response to a tone, for example. In Type II, as in my experiment, two reflexes are 'chained together' . . . and . . . remain in that relation (the lever is pressed and the pellet is eaten)."[16]

That we were studying very different processes became clear when we began to reinforce only intermittently. (This was the second time I could call myself Pavlov's contemporary.) Pavlov found it very hard to sustain salivation if food was not always paired with the conditioned stimulus, but rats pressed a lever rapidly and for long periods of time even though reinforcement was infrequent.

In many arrangements used to study conditioned leg flexion, the shock was terminated as the foot was lifted off the electrode. When the electrode was fastened to the foot, the leg presumably continued to flex until the experimenter terminate the shock, in which case similar contingencies prevailed. In 1936 Elmer Culler, one of those most active in studying the conditioned flexion reflex, gave a paper at the annual meeting of the American Psychological Association, at which I was asked to be a discussant. I again raised the question of the role of consequences. It seemed to me that the only possible example of a skeletal response fitting the Pavlovian formula was the patellar reflex studied by Schlosberg, but when I asked

---

[13]See H. D. Kimmel, "Notes from 'Pavlov's Wednesdays': Pavlov's law of effect," *American Journal of Psychology*, 89 (1976), 553–56.

[14]Ivan P. Pavlov, (London: Oxford University Press, 1927).

[15]B. F. Skinner, (New York: Knopf, 1979).

[16]B. F. Skinner, "On the rate of formation of a conditioned reflex," *Journal of General Psychology*, 7 (1932), 274–86.

Schlosberg about the role of consequences, he replied that they certainly had to be taken into account.

R. M. Church has pointed out that the conditioned emotional response studied by Watson and Rayner also involved consequences.[17] The rabbit and the loud noise were not paired; the noise occurred when Albert reached for the rabbit. The noise was better described as punishment. But it is possible that punishment works through the conditioning of aversive stimuli, and in any case autonomic responses were clearly involved.

In 1940 W. K. Estes and I studied a different kind of conditioned emotional reaction in what we called "anxiety."[18] We reinforced pressing a lever on a fixed-interval schedule until a stable performance was maintained. Midway during a session we sounded a tone for three minutes and then shocked the rat through the feet. Originally, neither the tone nor the shock seriously disrupted the performance, but slowly the behavior in the presence of the tone was suppressed. It is a very reliable effect and has been widely used. Brady and Hunt, for example, found that electroconvulsive shock, as well as tranquilizing drugs, eliminates the conditioned suppression. Although the tone no doubt elicits glandular and smooth-muscle responses, the suppression is not, strictly speaking, a conditioned reflex. *Conditioned reaction*, a broader term, might be used, but even so the effect does not fit the pattern of stimulus substitution, since no unconditioned stimulus produces the suppression. It is also possible that the conditioned salivation studied by Pavlov was not simply the salivation elicited by foodstuffs in the mouth transferred to an auditory stimulus; it could have been an innate response that would be elicited only when it became attached to a novel stimulus. See Chapter 5.

Although Pavlov's influence on experimental psychology was not great, various practices in behavior therapy have clearly been derived from his work. Desensitization is often no more than Pavlovian extinction. Curiously enough, Pavlov

---

[17]Russell M. Church, "The role of fear in punishment" in *Punishment*, ed. R. H. Walters, J. A. Cheyne, and R. K. Banks (Harmondsworth, England: Penguin 1972).

[18]William K. Estes and B. F Skinner, "Some quantitative properties of anxiety," *Journal of Experimental Psychology*, 29 (1941), 390–400.

has had a more profound effect upon amateur psychologists. Literary critics, political writers, and many others use the term *conditioned reflex* with abandon. Aldous Huxley was reasonably on target in *Brave New World*,[19] but it is not fair to call brainwashing "pavlovization." The popular usage often overrides the professional. Behaviorists have been victims of what might be called filial regression, as whatever they do is forced into the pattern of Pavlovian conditioning. Many years ago students in introductory psychology at Columbia worked with operant conditioning. The Columbia *Jester* published a cartoon showing two rats in a box, one of them saying to the other, "Boy, have I got this guy conditioned! Every time I press the bar down he drops in a piece of food." It was not long before the story was told this way: "Gee, have I got this fellow conditioned. Every time I *ring the bell* he gives me food." That is Pavlov's bell.

---

[19]Aldous Huxley, (New York: Harper & Row, 1932).

chapter 14

Some Thoughts about the Future

෴෴෴෴෴

In *The Shaping of a Behaviorist* I wrote that in 1947, looking back upon my research at Minnesota and Indiana, I saw that

> there had been a change in emphasis in my experimental work. When Garry Boring wrote to Mike Elliott to support my appointment at Minnesota, he said that I had been "sheltered" by five years of research fellowships. I was only just beginning to see an important effect. Almost all the experiments reported in *The Behavior of Organisms* were done to follow up leads arising from the work itself. I answered questions, clarified points, and solved practical problems raised by my own research. Once out of my shelter and in contact with other people, I turned to other questions: at Minnesota, how fast rats worked at maximal hunger, whether maze-bright and maze-dull rats differed in extinction, whether a rat could use tokens, and what effect drugs had on behavior; and at Indiana, reaction time, choice, and matching to sample. These were a kind of technological application of the operant methodology. I was *using* an experimental analysis of behavior rather than furthering it. The results were interesting to many more people, but they were digressions.[1]

---

[1]B. F. Skinner, (New York: Knopf, 1979), p. 343.

At Harvard, in collaborating with Charles B. Ferster, I returned to basics. But schedules of reinforcement proved almost too fascinating, and what I should have called central issues only occasionally broke through. Recently, in a brief return to the laboratory, I once again considered issues that came not from the research itself but from an application—to the simulation of so-called cognitive processes.

Our research on Project Pigeon during the Second World War was also a technological application of the operant analysis. My colleagues and I had to convince some very skeptical engineers that a living organism was at least as reliable as any other part of the missile they were working on. We did not convince the engineers, but we ourselves were more than satisfied with the control we achieved. One episode in particular made a great difference in later years. We discovered the ease with which we could shape the behavior of a pigeon simply by operating a reinforcing device with a hand switch at appropriate times.

I had been talking about control for many years, but now I began to do so in earnest. With a group of philosophers and literary critics I discussed many of the implications of a scientific analysis of human behavior. Much of *Walden Two* is little more than a rehash of those discussions. What the protagonist in *Walden Two* called a behavioral technology was at the time still science fiction, but it soon moved into the real world.[2] Curiously enough, there does not seem to have been a comparable interest in total control in basic research.

THE CONTROL OF BEHAVIOR

In the 1930s I was asking whether the behavior of a rat was determined, and if so, to what extent it could be predicted and controlled in an experimental space. If we could control all relevant conditions, could we explain *everything* the rat did? Some kinds of exceptional behavior are familiar. Adjunctive behavior is an example, and so is the emotional display seen during extinction—defecation in the case of the rat, and defe-

---

[2]B. F. Skinner, (New York: MacMillan, 1948).

cation, pacing, cooing, and ruffling of feathers in the case of the pigeon. Another example is the pigeon's occasional peck at some other feature of the apparatus ("displacement?"). Not quite unrelated to the experiment is a sharp turning away from the key, evidently a kind of escape that can be studied directly by installing a second key that stops the experiment briefly when pecked. We accept a certain amount of this, although it must affect our results. Can we eliminate it? One way, possibly not intentional, is to make intervals of rein-forcement so short or ratios so small that the pigeon responds very rapidly and has little time for anything else. But the resulting steep, straight lines that appear in so many reports lack interest and have almost been the death of the cumulative record.

In the 1930s I studied low rates. Knowing far less about why an organism behaves than I do now, I was content to see a few signs of lawful behavior against a background of "noise." I was impressed by the fact that a rat wandered about the box, sniffed in the corners, explored the ceiling, sat and scratched itself, and nevertheless went to the food tray and ate a pellet of food at just the right time to keep a satiation curve on its proper course. I gave exceptional behavior every chance and found a kind of order in spite of it. As we shall see, low rates of responding similar to those in most of *The Behavior of Organisms* may be essential if we are to observe certain complex interactions among the effects of controlling variables.[3]

The experimental chamber and its use in operant research is a kind of "preparation," like Sherrington's for the study of spinal reflexes or Thomas Hunt Morgan's for the study of genetics. A species of organism is chosen and a stan-dard space constructed. A corpus of facts about the organism is accumulated so that further research in a similar space need not start from scratch.

Certain features of the operant preparation are in danger of being lost. Much valuable research can be done in short periods of time on one or a few subjects. The experimenter can then watch the organism, observing features of its behavior

---

[3]B. F. Skinner, *The behavior of organisms,* (New York: Appleton-Century, 1938).

that are lost by the time the data reach a recorder. Closed-circuit television makes it easy to watch behavior without disturbing the organism, and video taping permits review.

Pigeons are highly suitable for a good preparation. We have already learned a great deal about them. Whether they are an adequate sample of organisms as a whole is questionable, of course, but we could even say the same thing of a hundred species when millions exist. The kind of pigeon, however, raises a problem. The Kings and White Carnaux usually found in the laboratory are not ideal. They are raised for squab meat and bred for weight, quick growth, efficiency in feeding their young, and good health in crowded quarters. They have lived in undemanding environments for many generations and may even have been selected against keen vision, good motor skill, and quick learning. Homing pigeons have been selected by more demanding contingencies and may be better subjects.

I am not sure that we have not made something of a fetish of *naive* pigeons. There are experiments in which they are necessary, of course, but sophistication has its advantages. There is something to be said for a pigeon that has been around a long time. A pigeon kept in a cage after hatching may be like a feral child. Charles Ferster and I used an old pigeon to test new circuits, and it became a kind of war horse that could put a new set of contingencies through its paces very quickly. It is true that some schedules have long-lasting effects, but perhaps a new setting takes total control more quickly after exposure to many settings. After all, the human subjects used in psychological research are not naïve, even though we often wish they were. When the question is simply whether a pigeon *can* exhibit a given pattern of behavior, sophistication is preferable to naïveté. A step-by-step construction of the pattern would have to begin with a naïve pigeon.

We can improve our control by improving daily care. A bit more living space, a controlled day-and-night light cycle, the use of only one sex to avoid incipient mating and brooding, a careful selection of food and grit, proper manicuring of beak and toes—all these should make for more uniform results.

The experimental space can also be improved. We are concerned with the behavior of a pigeon facing a panel bearing operanda, stimuli, and dispensers of reinforcers. The rest of the space should be as free as possible of eliciting and releasing stimuli. A cylindrical space would be better than a square one because it would have no odd corners to be explored. If the wall were transparent, the pigeon could be watched, either directly or with a video camera, through an opening in a larger, sound-absorbing enclosure.

The keys, with the usual standard specifications, should be set at a convenient height, and if different sizes of pigeons are used, the height should be adjusted. The pigeon should be able to reach reinforcers and drinking water without moving away from the panel. Most of the time a pigeon stands facing the panel because standing there is indirectly reinforced by the reinforcers in the experiment, but it will be more likely to remain there if additional contingencies are arranged. A small area in front of the panel that is especially comfortable for pigeon feet would help. After all, we use special contingencies to keep our human subjects in their places. (Those who complain of the artificiality of animal research, by the way, often seem to forget that the psychological laboratory is also far from the natural environment of the human species.)

When I was a graduate student, experiments in animal behavior were conducted in open rooms with the experimenter present and watching. Taking my cue from Pavlov, I put my first lever and reinforcer in a fairly soundproof room and later in a fairly soundproof box, but I worried about the effect of handling. In my first experiments, I put the rat first into a special section of the box, from which I released it (electrically and silently) after it had presumably recovered from being handled. Something of the sort should, I think, be standard practice. A sophisticated pigeon may not need time to recover from handling, but a naïve one certainly does. With pigeons, the box can be kept dark for a time. With animals that are active in the dark, the operandum and panel can be covered for a minute or two before the experiment starts.

Contingencies of reinforcement should be programmed with standard equipment, of course, and in many experiments the behavior is still most usefully recorded in cumulative records (especially when rates are low and curves are curved). Measures of interresponse times and on-line computer processing have their place, of course.

Circadian rhythms are important, and if we are to achieve anything like total control, they should be respected. Experiments should start at the same time every day in a seven-day week. That is not a feature of a preparation that appeals to everyone, but it is probably needed if we are to gain accurate control. Young workers may be willing to accept it, as I did, for the sake of the advantages.

The experiments described in the rest of this chapter can be carried out with a relatively simple preparation. They resemble, but go far beyond, the experiments I reported in *The Behavior of Organisms.* It is the kind of research in which something new and interesting turns up almost every day—in other words, research that is reinforced on a rich variable-ratio schedule.

Research of this kind also has economic advantages. It is much less expensive than research designed to test theories or to confirm principles. Budgets are getting smaller, and grants are always hard to get when agencies demand a clearer picture of potential results than is possible in truly exploratory research. One may try to impress granting agencies by giving one's work a broader significance. For example, most of what I shall describe could be called either the study of cognitive processes or, to use Pavlov's expression, "an investigation of the physiological activity of the cerebral cortex."[4] There is always the danger that a move in that direction will lead to digressions.

Cooperation with workers in other fields is often a useful source of support, however. We sometimes forget how far we have come as skilled craftsmen who can shape and maintain behavior to specification. When we speak of applied behavior analysis we usually mean analysis applied to human behavior in the world at large, but research with operant equipment

---

[4]I. P. Pavlov, *Conditioned reflexes: An investigation of the physiological activity of the cerebral cortex* (London: Oxford, 1927).

and methods in neurological and pharmacological laboratories is also applied and is often closer to basic research.

Here are some fields of operant research that I would look at closely if I were to return to the laboratory.

CHOICE

An organism is said to choose when it responds in a way that makes it impossible for another response to occur. All early animal research used choice—of pathways in mazes or of doors in discrimination boxes and jumping stands—as a measure of strength of response. Edward Tolman used a T-maze to study "behavior at a choice point." But the fact that a rat turns right rather than left or jumps to a circle rather than a square shows only that one response is stronger than another; it does not show how much stronger or yield an absolute measure of strength. Rate of responding comes much closer to doing this.

As I reported in *The Shaping of a Behaviorist*, when Tolman read *The Behavior of Organisms*, he wrote that I ought to put two levers in the box and "see what relationships the functions obtained from such a discrimination setup will bear to your purified functions where you have only one lever." When W. H. Heron and I built our twenty-four-box Behemoth, I wrote to Tolman that we had put in two levers and hoped to get around soon to some problems involving choice. Fortunately, we never made that mistake.

To return to choice and especially to regard a single response as a choice between responding and not responding are, I think, steps backward. Choice is something to be explained, not to be used in the analysis of basic processes. Its recent use in animal research may have been encouraged by similar treatments of human behavior. For the utilitarians, a choice was right if it promoted the greatest good for the greatest number; economists have appealed to the maximization of utility, as in the theory of subjective expected utility; and behavioral scientists speak of the optimization or melioration of other consequences.

Choice is needed only when there is no other measure of probability of responding. It is true that if a man does not do one thing, he will do another or do nothing, and that if you want him to do A and not B, you have only to make the "expected utility" of A greater than that of B, as by describing favorable consequences or reinforcing A more frequently. But in doing so you are changing only relative probabilities. Contingencies of reinforcement are much more powerful than the "expected utilities" that follow from instruction, and rate of responding is a more direct measure of probability than a choice between alternatives.

In a paper called "Are theories of learning necessary?" I reported some work on "behavior at a choice point" in which by occasionally reinforcing a response on one or the other of two keys without favoring either key, I obtained equal rates of responding. "The behavior approaches a simple alternation from one key to the other. This follows the rule that tendencies to respond eventually correspond to the probabilities of reinforcement."[5] That was an early statement of the matching law, but I hastened to add that

> the bird's behavior does not correspond to this probability merely out of respect for mathematics. The specific result of such a contingency of reinforcement is that changing-to-the-other-key-and-striking is more often reinforced than striking-the-same-key-a-second-time. [I was using an interval schedule.] We are no longer dealing with just two responses. In order to analyze "choice" we must consider a single final response, striking, without respect to position . . . of the key and in addition the response of changing from one key . . . to the other.

It is unlikely that a remote consequence of any kind can reinforce operant behavior in the absence of mediating events. When a schedule is suddenly changed so that the current rate of responding does not match the frequency of reinforcement, the behavior does not immediately change. Mediating processes must be conditioned before the new performance matches, and the conditioning is presumably the

---

[5]B. F. Skinner, "Are theories of learning necessary?" *Psychological Review*, 57 (1950), 193–216.

same as that which explains all schedule effects. It is also unlikely that remote consequences could have played any part in the evolution of the process of operant conditioning.

To return to choice after better measures of strength are available is like returning to the gas laws for information about the behavior of molecules after better ways of observing them have been discovered. The gas laws remain valid and useful, and so would laws about more general effects of contingencies if they could be proved.

STIMULUS CONTROL

We shall not achieve total control of operant behavior until we know more about the role of stimuli. Very early in my research I found it necessary to distinguish between what I called the discriminative stimulus in an operant and the eliciting stimulus in a reflex. I had been reinforcing a rat's behavior every five minutes, and when I began to turn on a light just as I set up a reinforcement, and off again immediately after a response, responding persisted in the presence of the light but disappeared in extinction in its absence. The term *discrimination* which I took from contemporary work on animal behavior, was not quite right. I did not really care whether a rat could tell the difference between light-on and light-off. The control acquired by a stimulus was the issue. I began to speak of a stimulus as "the occasion" for a response or even of responding "in" a stimulus as short for "in the presence of," but neither expression quite represents the way in which a stimulus gains control of an operant.

A related process that most people were calling *generalization* I called *induction*. Reinforcement "in light-on" generated some tendency to respond "in light-off." In Project Pigeon we found that after pecking a red triangle had been intermittently reinforced, the rate of pecking in extinction dropped when the triangle turned yellow. Guttman's work on stimulus generalization was, of course, a great clarification of that effect. Much more could be done to explore its relevance to "our knowledge of the world around us."

I tried to study induction by setting up a discrimination between two stimuli in the presence of one of which behavior had never been reinforced. As I reported in *The Behavior of Organisms*,

> at the release of the rat on the first day the light was on. A response to the lever occurred quickly and was reinforced. The light and magazine were then disconnected. . . . Only two responses were forthcoming during the next five minutes and it is difficult to say whether they show induction or were similar to [that is, occurred for the same reason as] the first response. When the light was turned on again, the rat responded after thirty-nine seconds. . . . Both light and magazine were then turned off, and two more responses in the dark occurred during the next five minutes.

During the rest of the session there were only two or three small groups of responses in the dark, and I noted that some of them could have been due to adventitious reinforcement by the appearance of the light.

Herbert Terrace took off from that experiment in his work on errorless discrimination learning. By building up an easy errorless discrimination between very different stimuli and then superimposing very similar stimuli on them and vanishing the originals, he taught his pigeons to distinguish between very similar stimuli without error. That a discrimination that was learned without errors produced no peak shift in the generalization gradient suggests that other riches lie unexplored in that field.

Another process, one that I called *reverse induction*, still puzzles me. Two of the eight rats in my experiment soon stopped responding altogether in the light as well as the dark, even though responses were always reinforced in the light. In a third rat, "inductive extinction nearly brought the series to an end in the last part of the second [period]." A rat would often wait nearly a minute before responding. The average latency during six hours was forty-one seconds. The average for all six rats was roughly three times that in my earlier experiments on discrimination. As far as I know, reverse induction has never been studied further, although it might throw unexpected light on "cognitive" processes and on puzzling problems in therapy.

REACTION TIME

Early in the history of psychology reaction time was taken as an important measure of the speed of mental processes, and cognitive psychologists are again using it as such. Differences in reaction time have even been said to reflect differences in intelligence, but if that is the case, it is surprising that, as I found many years ago, the reaction time for the pigeon is probably within the human range when the contingencies are properly programmed. Reaction times are only secondary properties of behavior, no doubt of value when we are guessing about what is going on inside the organism, but otherwise of interest only because complex cases are a challenge to the programmer of contingencies.

In the simplest case, a "ready" signal is given and after a short variable time a key is lighted and a response reinforced if it occurs within a given period, eventually to be measured in milliseconds. Initially a length of period is chosen in which reinforcement frequently occurs. The period is then progressively shortened as the pigeon responds more and more quickly. Responses made during the ready period turn the experiment off for a few seconds. Good waiting behavior eventually develops, but it can be quickly shaped if we end the ready period whenever the pigeon looks steadily at the key. When human subjects are told to "behave as fast as possible," the instruction presumably works because of similar contingencies in the subject's history, largely unknown to the experimenter. Because we must construct the pigeon's history, we know much more about it, and indeed about the role of reaction times in daily life.

Reaction-time experiments could occupy a researcher for a lifetime. How do the times differ when a response is reinforced only if the key is red and not if it is green? or when either a right or a left key is lighted? or when both keys are lighted but reinforcement is contingent on pecking the one that matches a color present during the ready period? or when a tone is used instead of a light? And so on. Skillful programming is needed, but that is what the experimental analysis of behavior is all about.

MULTIPLE OPERANTS

In one of the experiments I look back on with particular pleasure, William H. Morse and I used both water and food as reinforcers. There were three keys. Responses on one were intermittently reinforced with water, on another with food, and on the third with food or water unpredictably. The result was beautiful. As we changed the levels of deprivation of food and water, the rates on the respective keys changed, and the rate on the key to which responses were reinforced with food or water was always the average of the other two. It was a simple result but one that has vast implications for the field of "motivation."

An equally fascinating question is whether a pigeon can engage in more than one operant performance at the same time. Suppose we light the left of two keys and build up a steady low rate of pecking. In a separate session we build up a somewhat higher rate on the lighted right key, keeping the left key dark. Eventually, in a single session, the pigeon responds at a low rate whenever the left key is lighted and at a higher rate when the right key is lighted. On the critical day, both keys are lighted and the same schedules are in effect but with reinforcements out of phase. The time needed to consume the reinforcers should be negligible, and the two performances should run off essentially undisturbed. If there is any disruption, it will be what is right for the pigeon and what the experimenter must explain. In an interesting variation, responses on the left key could be reinforced with food and those on the right with water.

In Project Pigeon, Norman Guttman began an experiment in which a jacketed pigeon pecked a key but also pulled a string with one free leg. The experiment was unfinished when Guttman was called to his country's service. Something of the sort badly needs to be explored. An unjacketed pigeon might either peck a key or step on a treadle. Bring each response under appropriate stimulus control and then present both stimuli at the same time. The extent to which two or more operants can appear as parts of ongoing behavior without loss of stimulus control or confusion in topography is an extremely important question if we are ever to give a plausible account of behavior in the world at large.

SCHEDULES OF REINFORCEMENT

If Ferster and I had had another year or two to work together, we might have brought the analysis of schedules of reinforcement to a more satisfying state—though by no means to a conclusion. As I reported in *A Matter of Consequences*,

> We had a theory. Unless our pigeons had extrasensory perception (a suggestion we dismissed), they were in contact with the programming equipment only at the time of reinforcement. A number of stimuli were acting at the moment corresponding to readings on a speedometer (the bird had been responding at a given rate), a clock (a certain amount of time had passed since the last reinforcement), and a counter (a given number of responses had been made since the last reinforcement). We designed our experiments to give these stimuli a chance to make their presence known.[6]

One of our more surprising results came when we added counters, clocks, and speedometers to the keys the pigeons pecked. The instrumentation was crude. We projected a small bar of light on the key, the length of which changed with the number of pecks, elapsed time, or speed. We assumed that the bar and the internal stimulus changed in the same way, but it was soon clear that in general the bar was much stronger. As far as I know, this work has never been followed up, yet it could throw a great deal of light on why schedules have their

---

[6]B. F. Skinner, (New York: Knopf, 1983), pp. 73–74.

appropriate effects. It would be an alternative to current work in which much more elaborate contingencies of reinforcement can be programmed with an on-line computer.

BONUSES

As more control is achieved, other kinds of variables can be brought into an experiment at little or no extra cost. Bonuses are there for the asking. A few examples:

1. If we use two strains of pigeons (of both sexes), and if significant differences in their behavior appear, we can crossbreed and see what happens.
2. If we can arrange for the care of pigeons, we can put our subjects aside at the end of an experiment and bring them back a few years later to test for long-term "memory."
3. We can study the effects of diet far beyond anything possible with human subjects; vitamin deficiencies could be a starting point.
4. We can study visual processes in the pigeon with great precision, and there are diets and drugs that change the pigments in the pigeon's eye—another experimental manipulation that is out of reach of research on human subjects.

CONCLUSION

It is much easier to suggest experiments than to carry them out, and it is tempting to claim a discovery simply because one had said it *could* be made. But I am not staking claims; I am simply trying to recover the spirit of the research reported in *The Behavior of Organisms*. I think the experimental analysis of behavior can best proceed as it started, until the control of the behavior of an organism in an experimental space is very nearly total. A science of behavior will then have given neurology its clearest assignment, will have left nothing for cognitive science to explain with its mental operations, and will lead most rapidly to an effective technology of behavior in the world at large.

Acknowledgments

ଽ⧫ଽ⧫ଽ⧫ଽ⧫ଽ⧫

The chapters of this book were presented and published as indicated below. Permission to republish is gratefully acknowledged.

1. Presented: American Psychological Association, August 1982.
2. Presented: American Psychological Association, August 1985. Published: *American Psychologist* (May 1986).
3. Published: *The Behavior Analyst*, 8 (Spring 1985), 5–14.
4. Published: *Science*, 213 (31 July 1981), 501–4. Copyright © 1981 by the American Association for the Advancement of Science.
5. Copyright © 1984 by the Society for the Experimental Analysis of Behavior, Inc. Originally published in *Journal of the Experimental Analysis of Behavior*, 41 (1984), 217–21.

Index